*f*P

The Managerial Moment of Truth

The Essential Step
in Helping People
Improve Performance

Bruce Bodaken and Robert Fritz

Foreword by Peter Senge

FREE PRESS
NEW YORK   LONDON   TORONTO   SYDNEY

*f*P

FREE PRESS
A Division of Simon & Schuster, Inc.
1230 Avenue of the Americas
New York, NY 10020

For information about special discounts for bulk purchases,
please contact Simon & Schuster Special Sales:
1-800-456-6798 or business@simonandschuster.com

Designed by Karolina Harris

Manufactured in the United States of America

10 9 8 7 6 5 4 3 2 1

Library of Congress Cataloging-in-Publication Data
Bodaken, Bruce.
The managerial moment of truth: the essential step in helping people improve performance / Bruce Bodaken and Robert Fritz; foreword by Peter Senge.
p. cm.
1. Personnel management. 2. Performance—Management. I. Fritz, Robert. II. Title.
HF5549 .B75815   2006
658.3'14—dc22   2005058937

ISBN-13: 978-0-7432-8852-1
ISBN-10:   0-7432-8852-1

For Dad, Mike, Conor, and Ian. You are the source and inspiration for wanting to make a difference while I'm here. Your love has made it safe to try.

—BRUCE BODAKEN

To you, Rosalind. Your truth telling shatters illusions and shows the beauty of reality. You are a wonder.

—ROBERT FRITZ

Contents

Foreword
Peter M. Senge

Performance problems invariably throw managers into a bind. "Should I tell this person what I really think about his performance or should I not hurt his feelings or say something that will demotivate him?" Indeed, there are plenty of dangers on all sides. Not talking openly about performance issues often guarantees that they will not improve. On the other hand, "being straight" with people can easily backfire as well.

I was speaking recently with a good friend guiding a huge "cultural integration" effort brought about by a Fortune 50 company's acquisition of an almost equally large business, and she was commenting on destructive dynamics playing out between the two companies. "They have a culture of what they call 'open feedback,' which we experience as rude and closed-minded. They are fond of telling people what they really think about each other's performance, but it seems they are rarely open to questioning their interpretations. They select the data that make their point, then deliver 'their truth' based on their selected data. If you differ with them, they tend to accuse you of not wanting to face the facts. We have spent years trying to build a culture of mutual respect and integrity, but they often see this as people just being 'nice' to each other, which they worry compromises business performance."

Today, many organizations are trying to build values-based cultures, seeing values such as integrity and honesty as important not only to staying out of trouble but also to building innovative and high-performing cultures. But experience suggests that most of these efforts are unlikely to succeed. I would expect that both of the companies entangled in the cultural integration described above see themselves as "values-based." Probably each questions the values of the other. Having a debate about their respective cultures and value sets would probably make things worse, not better. In fact, both are caught in a simpler, and deeper, issue: *How do we speak the truth to one another in ways that work?* There are few more fundamental challenges in management, from the boardroom to the shop floor.

Having watched countless organizations struggle with this core question for a long time, I believe *The Managerial Moment of Truth* is an elegant method that could have a significant impact:

- acknowledging present reality;
- examining people's thinking about how it got to be that way;
- creating a plan for what needs to change;
- establishing a feedback system to track improvement against that plan.

On the surface, the elements look simple, but doing them well consistently is no mean feat.

As the above story illustrates, coming to shared agreement as to what constitutes "present reality" often is not trivial. It is easy for each party in any conflict to see their view of reality as "the truth" and never question whether there are other data that might equally define the truth or differing legitimate interpretations of the same data. Carrying out this very first step well requires a real willingness to inquire, rather than simply imposing your own view of things absolutely. People also avoid coming to agreement about the present state because the present state may include aspects about which people are embarrassed, angry, or anxious. So, acknowledging present reality well also involves a willingness to deal with emotional conflicts.

Examining our thinking about how reality came to be as it is can be equally challenging. In simple situations there may be a straightforward view that different parties can agree to, although again there may be strong emotions associated with people's assessments. But, as Bodaken and Fritz show, in complex situations this rarely is so, and people's assessments may range from "he or they let me down" to "our system is screwed up." For example, my MIT colleague Nelson Repenning has shown that companies often get caught in perpetual "firefighting": they struggle with getting products to market on time, then throw resources at late projects and divert them from ones "further upstream" (i.e., further from launch). Caught in the middle of this syndrome, managers inevitably have compelling circumstantial reasons why their project is behind schedule and needs more money to complete. Executives feeling the heat of meeting launch targets grudgingly comply. But in taking resources from upstream projects not in crisis, important early design work gets shortchanged, thereby guaranteeing more late projects in the future. Neither party sees their part in a deeper pattern perpetuating the cycle of firefighting and underinvestment in the early stages of projects.

People often have very different views of causality, and our views are often self-serving. Coming to a shared interpretation of performance shortfalls requires openness to share these views and inquire into the reasoning that supports them. It requires openness to different views that may come from "outsiders," such as newcomers to the company not yet caught in managers' established mental models. But, as with our selection of data, people are mostly used to advocating their interpretations rather than inquiring into them and challenging them. The Nobel laureate physicist Richard Feynman once said that "the scientist's greatest responsibility is to disprove his own theories." Yet few scientists, if pressed, would pass this test, let alone those of us less rigorously trained in critical reasoning. Examining people's thinking well requires mutual openness and trust, and as Bodaken and Fritz say, a genuine love of the truth. Put simply, getting to the truth must be more important than feeling comfortable and protecting our egos.

The Managerial Moment of Truth invites us to develop a discipline of truth telling. The first prerequisite for a discipline is method. The pages that follow lay out an elegant method that has great potential. But make no mistake. Discipline goes beyond tools. It requires tools combined with commitment, and here is where many individuals and organizations falter. As one of my managerial mentors once put it, "I go all around the world talking to people about building organizations based upon openness, trust, and commitment to the truth, and everyone seems to want to work in this sort of an environment. But if this is true, it raises a real question. If everyone truly values such work environments, why are they so rare? I have come to the conclusion that people have little idea of the nature of the commitment that building such an environment requires."

It is easy to embrace the logic of a method like *The Managerial Moment of Truth*. It is easy to be attracted to its legitimate potential for significant performance improvement. But as the authors well understand, practicing it diligently requires genuine personal commitment to a level of reflectiveness and vulnerability that few organizations exhibit, and if anything seems to be becoming less common in today's high-pressure work environments. When the heat is on and there are difficult issues to confront, when I am part of the problem and cannot simply blame it on somebody or something else, that simple question—"*Is* getting to the truth more important than feeling comfortable?"—becomes truly "a moment of truth."

Lastly, as shown below, this work is all about teams and therefore relationships. In fact, individuals will consistently shy away from this work if they do not feel trusted or know they can trust others, if they feel that they alone must be the open ones. In order to become self-reinforcing and self-sustaining, commitment to the truth must be mutual.

This is especially true for managers. Because you are in a hierarchical position of authority, your own behavior is highly visible. "We cannot hear your words; your actions speak too loudly" goes an old saying. Nowhere is this truism more apt than for learning processes that involve personal vulnerability and openness. Do not expect others to implement what you yourself do not. Do not become an advocate for others to change their behavior. Become a practitioner of the managerial moment of truth yourself and ask others around you to help you be a good one.

If you are not ready for this, I recommend you set this book aside, because this is not a book with just a bunch of "good ideas." It is a call to a simple but transformative practice, one vital to building an organization truly worthy of people's highest commitment.

Preface

Truth is a tricky subject in any context. People rightly ask, what *is* the truth? How do we know? Are we really talking about truth or opinion? Isn't it dangerous to tell people the truth? Can they take it? Might we harm people by telling them the truth?

These are good questions, and that's why we want to clearly define the areas we are addressing before asking you to dive into a book entitled *The Managerial Moment of Truth*.

What do we mean by *truth* in this book? How can we learn to see and then communicate what is true, and do so in ways that are positive, productive, practical, helpful, and effective?

Before answering these important questions, let us make this claim: *truth is one of the most important competitive advantages there is in building a business*. Truth is the most vital element an organization has in fostering collective learning. When we are able to explore and then tell each other the truth, we can improve performance, both individually and collectively.

Imagine trying to build an organization without the ability to tell each other the truth. We would not be able to correct mistakes, learn from past performances, adjust our processes, and better understand the reality in which we are engaged. In fact, a glaring statistic is that over 50 percent of businesses fail within their first three years. The reason they fail is that they don't know what is going on in reality, which may include their financial position, their impact on the market-place, the nature of their customers' real motivations, and other key factors. Had they known the truth, they would have had a far greater chance of success. Without perceiving reality, it is next to impossible to succeed because invariably decisions are made in a vacuum.

There are many steps for improving performance: training, creating reinforcing reward systems, instituting effective computer systems, holding offsite planning meetings, developing the right hiring practices, and so on. Each step has its place in creating better performance, but the managerial moment of truth is the *essential* step that makes all the others work. Unless reality is penetrated, very little significant improvement can occur. It's sad to see time and energy invested in performance improvement, only to have it thwarted by what is missing in action—people speaking truthfully and honestly with one another. That is the indispensable step in any organization that hopes to achieve greater capability, professionalism, and alignment.

Some would argue that human beings are incapable of objectivity because of the nature of perception, which they see as idiosyncratic. We can understand the world only through our senses, which we then interpret. We are left with opinion at best, and, therefore, no one is right or wrong.

These ideas are interesting, but they don't hold up to scrutiny. If we look to the aural realm of a musical pitch, we can see how universal human perception is, because not only can we hear the pitch that is sounding, we can also see it on an oscilloscope. If two musicians are playing out of tune with each other, most people can hear the dissonance. Yet even if they are tone deaf, they can see the actual waveform the dissonance creates on an oscilloscope. In a discipline like music, people don't talk about "my pitch [truth], and your pitch [truth]" when they have to play together. There is an objective reality they can understand, and because of that objectivity, more than one hundred people can play together in a symphony orchestra and all play in tune.

In this book we talk about truth (small *t*) as objective, factual, and observable. A due date was made on time or it wasn't. The performance was adequate or it wasn't. The numbers are the numbers.

We also talk about areas that are not so clear-cut, questions that may be subject to differing opinions, such as acceptable levels of quality, personal alignment within a team, one's capabilities, skills, or attitude. *What is important is the spirit of inquiry we adopt.* We see the process as one of pursuing, as best we can, the actual reality under consideration.

We are not content with simply sharing impressions or opinions. With what rigor do we seek to understand reality, even if what we find contradicts our pet theories, our years of experience, our outlook, philosophy, or worldview? Our personal notions notwithstanding, *what is the actual reality and how do we know it?*

The managerial moment of truth approach is one of mutual exploration and learning. Together, we are backing up and studying reality. "Are you seeing what I'm seeing? Am I seeing what you are seeing? And where we are seeing reality differently from each other, how are we to understand why we are seeing it differently?" Rather than fight about who is right and who is wrong, together we are dedicating ourselves to observing reality and trying to better understand what we are seeing.

The old chestnut of the blind men and the elephant suggests that we can't explore reality, only piece together differing opinions, all of which are valid.

In case you haven't heard the original story for a while, here it is: Four blind men encountered an elephant. They began to reach out to touch the elephant to understand its shape. One blind man, who found the elephant's tail, said, "An elephant is like a rope!" "No," said another, who put his arms around the legs, "an elephant is like a tree trunk." "Nonsense," said another, who found the elephant's trunk, "the elephant is like a hose." Still another one of the men touched the elephant's tusks. "The elephant is like large teeth."

But when we think about it, shouldn't we rename the story "The Stupid Blind Men and the Elephant"? After all, these people were arguing about each person's perception, but they weren't asking each other how it came to pass that they had such vastly different ideas. The story is meant to tell us that everyone has a piece of the truth. Even though we may have vastly different ideas, they all reflect an aspect of reality. Perhaps. But an elephant is more than something like a rope, a tree trunk, a hose, and big teeth. These are but elements that are seen from a fragmented and limited point of view. I may have wheels, doors, seats, and an engine, and yet I may not have a car. To understand that we are considering a car, we need to see the gestalt—the parts in relationship to the whole.

Let's change the story to "The Smart Blind Men and the Elephant." In this story, one of the blind men says, "An elephant seems like a tree trunk," and his friends say, "Okay, keep feeling around and then report what it's like." Over time, the team would be able to describe what an elephant is like by sharing their insights and then further exploring the parts of the elephant they haven't yet encountered.

In management, truth telling too often has come to mean simply sharing opinions. This is not what truth telling means in this book. Trading opinions doesn't usually lead to greater understanding. What's missing is *the discipline to understand the foundation of various opinions.* We do that by measuring conclusions against reality. When we are objective, we don't pick only the facts that support our opinions to the exclusion of facts that don't. We are able to look at everything and allow ourselves to change our minds, alter our impressions, and abandon outdated ideas for ones that fit the facts.

Most of us have been taught to study reality in relationship to our theories, experiences, concepts, ideals, and so on. The thought process then is one of comparison. We compare reality against our ideas about reality. This approach limits our ability to see those things that are inconsistent with our previous notions. When we think we know all the answers, we don't ask targeted questions that enable us to explore new territory. But if we look anew, without presuming we know the answers to questions under consideration, we can discover new insights and relationships, rethink our assumptions, and go well beyond our basic suppositions. This book explores ideas about how we can look more carefully and see reality for what it is. Seeing reality objectively requires a large degree of rigor. Within the context of the organization, it also requires a process of collective inquiry. How can we bring people into the process? How can we consistently be willing to look at the hard facts? What would motivate us to strive for greater understanding, even when the exploration shines light on our own failings? How can we become better at our jobs and profession? How can we do that as a team and a company?

Telling the Truth

Unearthing the truth accurately is one thing. Telling it is yet another thing entirely. The classic line that reflects many managers' reservations to call it like it is comes from the film *A Few Good Men* when the Jack Nicholson character says, "You can't *handle* the truth." Most of us have the general impression that the unabashed truth is hurtful and devastating. We have grown up in a society that agrees with the Jack Nicholson character. Yet study after study has shown quite an opposite story. When there is a choice between knowing the unvarnished truth or not, people would rather know than be in the dark. Psychological studies consistently show that those who are in command of the facts are healthier than those who are not. One such study demonstrated that teenage pregnant girls who were flat out rejected by their families were more able to deal with their situation in a healthier and more productive way that those who, in fact, were rejected but never told that directly. The fact is we need to know where we stand with each other, not only teens in trouble, but managers from every level of the organization. Can people handle the truth? The resounding answer is Yes!

Having said that, we need to talk about the real world. The idea here is not just to tell the truth, but to have the telling of it be productive and helpful, and to lead to a positive change in the future. Telling the truth certainly involves a recitation of facts. But there is much more to communication than some clinical and cold statement of information. Motive makes a difference. What are we after? What do we want to accomplish? What type of relationship do we want with the people we work with? The book will explore these critical questions extensively and shed light on major distinctions that can make all the difference between long-term success and just a short-term improvement followed by regression into past unproductive patterns.

We need to make a clear distinction between attempting to manipulate a person and making a potentially tough conversation as accessible as we can make it.

The attempt to control the inner experience of another person to get him to do what we want him to do is the aim of manipulation. The underlying assumption here is that the person, left to his own devices, would not want to accomplish the goals. And because of that, the manager needs to *make* the person fall into line. Whether through charm or threats, the manager sees the job as getting a person to do what he hasn't freely chosen to do.

Managers can't build capacity through a manipulative approach because people react by becoming less self-generating. At best they can comply with directives. They cannot truly align with the direction leadership has chosen. This creates profound limitations to growth, development, and advancement for everyone.

If we think people can't handle the truth, we soften it. That's a manipulation. Or we sneak in the harsh facts between a series of compliments. That's a manipulation. Or we try to instill the fear of wrath to create a sense of urgency. That, too, is a manipulation. Manipulation can work to produce favorable results short-term. Long-term the strategy backfires. Manipulation is one of the worst management approaches anyone can take because it undermines a sense of relationship and credibility between the manager and the person managed.

Yet too often managers feel they have no other choice if they are to be true to their accountabilities. So with the best of intentions, they try to find out what the market will bear and then play the game for all it's worth. The limitations to this approach are these: you can't build capacity over time, and you can't build real relationships with the people you manage.

Manipulation harms relationships. This statement is true in every type of relationship from the most intimate to the most professional.

Rather than a sense of authentic relationship, people develop counterstrategies such as *don't show all your cards, hold back some level of involvement, don't care,* and *avoid truthfulness.* Under these circumstances people pretend to have true relationships, but they are simply playing the hand they feel was dealt them. In an unfair game, no one plays fairly.

Telling the truth means finding a platform from which to tell it. Not everyone takes in information the same way. As managers, we need to be sensitive to how best to tell the truth. For example, if we are talking to the chief financial officer, we can easily run through the accounts. But if we need to talk about the numbers with someone not steeped in accounting disciplines, we may have to alter what we say, how we explain it, how quickly we can move through information, and so on. Our change in approach is not a manipulation. Instead, we are varying our approach because we understand that this person cannot understand the financial content we are communicating as easily as would an expert. When it comes to truth telling within the organization, we want to be sensitive to how the person to whom we are talking takes in information, but we never want to soften the truth. We want to make the truth understandable, accessible, and comprehensive. We want to join with the person in an exploration of how the situation is, how it got to be that way, and how we can do better next time.

As managers, we try to find ways to better communicate to those with whom we work. The techniques in this book are not designed as prepackaged routines with which managers "process" people. We will describe a particular process we encourage managers to use. But we encourage each manager to apply the techniques in ways that are consistent with the situations she faces. We will present a four-step form, but the form itself comes alive when a manager in the real world applies it to a particular situation with real people. This book presumes that professional managers bring with them critical judgment, thoughtfulness, and practicality. A manager will know how and when to use the techniques in the heat of battle.

The musical form of the blues has a fixed structure. Baseball has a fixed structure. Other forms in the arts and in sports have fixed structures. Yet the forms are only the frame for the unique, creative, vital experience that people make of these forms. The same is true for the form we propose in this book. It is not designed to be some rigid tool that is used without regard to the actual people and situations we face. Instead, we offer the techniques in the book to be adopted in the spirit of what you bring to it—your own intelligence, professionalism, good sense, and humanity.

The written page doesn't give us the tonal context we would need to fully understand the spirit in which something is said. We need to hear the sound of the voices to understand the true feeling tone. The book contains dialogues in which harsh facts are spoken. Often truth contains unpleasant facts, instances of failures, disappointments, and confusion. While the words can seem harsh, the tonality we would like your mind's ear to hear is positive, helpful, objective, and supportive even while being frank. This book, if read without the sense of humanity we intend it to have, can sound too severe at times. We are not in favor of abusing people by using the truth as an excuse to beat them up. We are in favor of telling people the unvarnished truth in ways that are accessible, kind, and supportive.

It is *not* supportive to distort reality just so people do not have to feel badly about situations they have managed. Of course, we feel badly when we do not succeed. But feeling badly comes with the territory of being a professional who is reaching to accomplish goals that are not always within one's means. It's appropriate to feel badly when the situation calls for it. Yet our motive for improving isn't simply to restore a feeling of equilibrium. Rather, it is *because* we want to do a better job, succeed for ourselves, the team, and the organization that we are willing to face the truth, feel whatever we feel, and figure out what we can learn to improve next time out.

The scope of the book includes the individual, work teams, cross-discipline teams, senior management, subcontractor relationships, and strategic alliances. How can we use moments of truth to improve our performance, productivity, and creativity? How can we work better together? What is the role of the manager in this process? How can the manager enable others to change for the better? These are the critical questions that this book addresses.

Instead of using the often awkward *his and her*, we will sometimes use *his* and sometimes *her*. We are addressing both genders in either case.

The phrase *managerial moment of truth* will be used to describe events in which the manager has a choice to ignore or call attention to what has occurred. We will use *MMOT* to describe the technique we suggest to address such moments of truth. The book is aimed at managers from the most senior levels to those who work on the line. A manager may have a direct report who is also a manager. The use of the term *manager* in the book is universal and is not intended to suggest a form of managerial class system. In fact, it is our suggestion that managerial moments of truth can be initiated top-down, laterally, down-up, and across functions.

It is our intention to bring an approach to the manager and the organization that can revolutionize how we work together, think together, and create our future together. The subject of truth, particularly within the organization, is enormously challenging. But it is also extraordinarily worthwhile, positive, and practical. Today, organizations are faced with sudden shifts in marketplace realities, migrating economics, and the lightning speed of globalization. The organizations that can deal with these changing realities have the best prospect of survival. Those organizations that cannot "handle the truth" will be left in the dust. Learning how to tell each other the truth, as hard a discipline as it is within the organization, will make all of the difference.

Introducing the Managerial
Moment of Truth Approach

This book is about a critical technique called the Managerial Moment of Truth (MMOT). When managers understand and use this practice, they can add anywhere from 25 to 40 percent more actual capacity to their organizations without adding significant cost. It is one heck of a technique.

This is not an empty claim. Much of the insight presented in this book was developed within the context of a larger leadership approach that coauthor Bruce Bodaken initiated as part of a major change management effort for Blue Shield of California.

Blue Shield of California was the beta site for MMOT. By 2004 all managers (more than 400 people) and 25 percent of staff (more than 600 people) were trained in the use of this technique. Because it is a concrete methodology that helps people focus on management development, the MMOT approach added a unique new dimension to people's leadership. The proof of this pudding is found in significantly improved performance. Blue Shield of California is one of the fastest-growing health-care providers in the state, and by 2005 it transformed itself from a $3 billion legacy company five years before, to a $7 billion-plus progressive organization leading change within the health-care industry.

The Managerial Moment of Truth technique was developed by coauthor Robert Fritz to better implement Bruce's idea that certain critical leadership principles and behaviors need to be disseminated among management at every level within the organization.

Here is how Bruce described the organization in December 2003:

> As in many other organizations, Blue Shield of California was filled with managers that often didn't take the time to analyze the management component of chronic underperformance. This was especially true when reality included harsh facts. It was common to habitually soften the truth to prevent offending someone. Even worse, we would avoid mentioning mistakes, missed dates, less than acceptable quality, ineffective work habits, and a host of other inadequate performance standards when we saw them. The exception to this rule was when the situation was especially bad. Then the manager would overreact. The long-term impact was a temporary reaction, but not real and lasting change.

Of course, given this situation, it was difficult to improve performance significantly.

Too often, managers think they have only one of two unpleasant choices: to have a contentious confrontation or to avoid addressing the situation. Whichever path they choose, real and lasting change rarely happens.

This book presents a better approach. It enables managers to recognize reality as it is *early on* and effectively address those things that need adjustment. This technique enables the organization to develop a culture of continuous improvement, ongoing learning, and ever-increasing personal and team capacity.

Any good or great organization has integrity as a baseline value, so there's zero tolerance for intentional deception. If the organization isn't acting proactively on that front, dishonesty in the organization will thrive and the results will be disastrous. The Enrons of the world notwithstanding, most organizations do have baseline integrity. If you're outright lying and get caught at it, there are certain to be severe consequences.

But there's another type of dishonesty that's found in the cultural norms of the organization. Many organizations do have a subtle level of deceitfulness in which managers adopt implicit collective rules such as *never argue with the boss*, or *never admit your own mistakes*, or *don't question data*, or *lower your goals so you won't fail*. The MMOT can address these cultural norms by giving us a form in which we can explore the various assumptions we make—cultural, strategic, business, market, statistics, and so on. It also can show us where there are conflicts of competing values and conflicts of interests so we can know what decisions we need to make.

We can't enable people to overcome their organizational cultural blind spots by decree. But we can use a process of rigorous inquiry to explore the underpinnings of norms that distort reality. Inevitably a new foundation will be created by our exploration, because the old one cannot withstand scrutiny.

If you're a strong leader, you want people around you to tell you the hard truth. You want to be able to tell the people around you the hard truth as well. When asked to name the "secret to success for the organization," without missing a beat, Jack Welch said, "Candor." Of course, he is right. But just asking people to tell you the truth doesn't mean they will. If candor is truly the secret to success, why is it so rare? We need to learn how to tell the truth to each other, which isn't the same as spouting our opinions and sharing our feelings. Many managers who have lived through the last several decades have had to participate in group meetings in which people insulted each other for hours on end in the name of "honesty." These types of sessions are the opposite of seeking and telling the truth. They could be called opinion dumps, because telling someone your opinion is not the same as exploring reality. Groups that really tell each other the truth are the ones that ask each other questions, seriously seek to understand opinions that are different from their own. They strive to comprehend rather than simply impose their ideas on others, and they engage in a collective dialogue in which people together seek understanding.

Telling the truth begins by seeing reality for what it is without the distorting lens of our bias, concepts, theories, speculations, or past experiences. We can begin to study reality by presuming to *not* know what we might find, rather than start out presupposing we know all the answers. As managers and leaders, we need to develop the discipline of rigorous questioning, looking for how reality actually is, even if it forces us to change our opinions or assumptions. We need to grow a culture of honesty in which people can face reality together, dig deeper than was their habit, and commit themselves to facing reality, even when it's hard and uncomfortable to do so.

It is not easy to build such a culture. We need both method and commitment. We need tools that enable us to explore reality far beyond our beliefs and opinions. We need to connect with our own dynamic urge for truth. We need to do this as individual and team practitioners. The MMOT is an elegant approach in which we can put these building blocks in place within an organization.

The technique is based on four basic factors: the manager's ability to see the unvarnished reality, the manager's ability to bring people into a process of analyzing that reality, then creating a better designed managerial approach for the future, and finally establishing a system of follow-through as a mentoring process for improved performance.

Reality is an acquired taste. Like all acquired tastes, at first it may seem strange or even bitter. But as time passes and experiences build, we begin to appreciate and then hunger for it. Once an organization acquires a taste for reality, it is hard to go back to anything that is less accurate, truthful, and clean.

The Work-arounds

When busy managers don't know how to address substandard work, typically they develop work-arounds. The most common is giving a bigger role to the high performers in the team and underutilizing those whose work patterns need improvement.

If you recognize yourself in this description, you're not alone. Most managers in most organizations shift the workload to the high performers. When you're a busy manager with accountabilities you take seriously, it is natural to bypass the less accomplished managers.

Who has the time to put in the needed corrections? Yet if you don't take the time, you will always be in a situation in which you lack the capacity you need.

THEY'RE NOT BAD ENOUGH

The less accomplished people we are talking about are often capable. Few are bad enough to fire, but many are not good enough to assign important work. By avoiding assigning the more challenging work to these people, you are straining the entire team. The better performers begin to experience burnout, while the less accomplished folks feel undervalued, disrespected, and unable to roll up their sleeves and get involved.

This pattern happens over time. We can find ourselves building a large degree of resentment and frustration as the cycle continues without significant improvement. The cumulative work-arounds take their toll. One day we may find ourselves blowing up over something small, some little mistake, some innocent miscommunication, the same behavior we seemed to have tolerated for a long time.

Since the reaction is disproportionate to the actual gaffe, most people think we are having a bad day, having trouble at home, or having a chemical reaction to something we ate. The punishment doesn't fit the crime, and everyone, including us, knows it.

The explosion doesn't lead to change. Instead, the heat of the moment passes and you and the person are embarrassed. Having expressed your anger and frustration, you no longer feel the same degree of conflict you were feeling. The storm passes, and both of you pretend it never happened.

TOO LITTLE/TOO MUCH/TOO LITTLE

This is a pattern we call *Too Little/Too Much/Too Little*. For a long time, you do too little to correct the work habits of the people you manage. Over time, the emotional tension grows as you try to deal with your very heavy workload. Added to that, there are too few people you can count on. Then one day, the straw that breaks the camel's back happens and in a flash you overreact.

Frankly, your reaction is not motivated by an altruistic desire to mentor a manager who needs to better develop his management technique. Nor are you trying to shock him into managerial enlightenment. You simply can't stand it anymore. Even though you wanted to restrain yourself, your tolerance failed you. And suddenly it's a managerial war zone.

After the episode is over, the situation regresses to *Too Little* again. Except that now you are convinced you are stuck in an untenable situation. Since the person is not bad enough to get fired, yet not good enough to use for important work, you feel trapped. In such situations, people tend to blame others rather than explore how they might be contributing to suboptimal performance.

THE TIME FACTOR

Usually busy people think they can't take the time to work with a weaker or inexperienced manager. However, the fact is, if they don't help these people improve, they will spend more time on work-arounds than they would have if they had addressed performance issues properly in the first place.

The work-arounds make matters worse because they are a short-term fix of a symptom triggered by a chronic cause, not a workable strategy designed to increase a team's performance. The person in need of improvement might not know there is a need for him to improve. The situation gets worse because it is left to fester.

On the other hand, if you learn the techniques presented in this book, you will find a very small investment of time dramatically improves the situation. Part of the approach is to recognize what's going on and to intervene when the symptom first shows, when it is easy to address—well before the situation grows into a more difficult management muddle.

PLANTING THE SEEDS OF CONFRONTATIONS

Most people hate to confront others. They avoid it at all costs. Ironically, by avoiding correcting performance that needs adjustments *early* in the managerial process, they plant the seeds of a real confrontation down the line. The techniques we will lay out in this book use this principle:

Make corrections when they are small and insignificant, well before they become a chronic bad habit that demands a full confrontation.

If you truly want to avoid confrontation, nip it in the bud by learning how to have critical moments of truth with the people you manage when the situation calls for it. If you take this advice, here are some of the advantages you will enjoy:

- a mentoring relationship with the people you manage;
- a way to build your capacity without adding cost;
- a way for the team to learn together;
- a larger capacity for truth being addressed objectively and fairly;
- your team learning how to become more objective in their self-evaluation;
- working with people who can admit their mistakes and short-comings, and can learn from them;
- a system for continuous improvement;
- the ability to rethink and redesign management processes and strategies;
- the ability for you to improve as an effective leader.

In organizations that build the MMOT into the management approach, the orientation shifts and the culture changes. Some of the most useful and dramatic shifts are around truth.

In many organizations, people manage the news and everyone knows it. If managers spin, editorialize, distort, avoid, and thwart any semblance of an honest look at reality, especially when the facts are troublesome, the subtext is "Don't tell the truth when the news is bad."

Some organizations have reward systems that in effect coax people to lie but punish people if they tell the truth when reality is problematic. Those who point out the more unpleasant facts fail to get promotions, are exiled to the boondocks, and do not win friends and influence people.

People need to know they *can* be honest within the organization. Too often, the undertone within many organizations is, "Tell the boss what she wants to hear." This norm makes it hard for the boss to get needed information.

When people can't address reality directly, they find other, unproductive ways of voicing their grievances. The escape valve becomes the hallway gripe session, in which people vent their frustrations fruitlessly.

When you make a place for managers to tell the truth to each other, good things begin to happen. Everyone feels, well, "cleaner." People begin to find that they can rely on each other. They can share their impressions with each other, discuss and sort out discrepancies, and learn how to learn together. In a fair game, people will play fairly, and the MMOT sets up a fair game, one in which people can succeed, grow, and win.

1
Basic Techniques:
Mastering the Fundamental Form
for Managerial Truth Telling

For every manager there are critical moments that occur regularly. These moments often go unnoticed, and yet they will determine the manager's destiny. We call these *managerial moments of truth*.

The way you deal with these moments will either trap you in a cycle of limitations making your work life harder, or enable you to unleash crucial capacity, align your team, and increase the impact of your leadership.

The Actual Moment of Truth

The actual moment of truth consists of two distinct events.

The first event is your *awareness* that there is a difference between what you expected and what was delivered. The second is the *decision* you make about what to do with that information.

Awareness is followed by a decision to address or ignore the event. Whatever you decide, a managerial moment of truth has happened. This is a defining moment, because the decisions you make will determine your impact as a manager. Moreover, the typical pattern of those decisions will establish the norms you set for your direct reports, the broader team, and the organization as a whole.

A missed due date is a moment of truth, as is an incomplete project or an unacceptable quality of work. If you consistently handle these types of moments of truth well, you will be leading your team to higher performance, increased learning, and deeper alignment.

On the other hand, if you manage them poorly, you are teaching your team many unfortunate lessons that will come back to haunt you, such as:

- It's okay for people to turn in a less than excellent performance.
- It's okay for people to fall short of expectations as long as they have a good excuse.
- It's okay for people NOT to do what they said they were going to do.

If you choose to address the situation, you are putting yourself, the people involved, and the entire team in a position to grow, develop, improve, and rethink their overall managerial process. If you turn away from an MMOT, you are impeding the team's future performance and your own managerial credibility. And yet most of us find it easier to ignore a moment of truth than address it. Why?

The underlying dynamic is that as human beings we want to avoid discomfort, embarrassment, confrontation, and emotional conflict, our own and that of others. We may tell ourselves we are too busy to spend time addressing the situation; that we can more easily and quickly do the work ourselves; or that this is a good performer, and we don't want to discourage her over such little things.

We may have attempted to make corrections when the situation called for it, but our past attempts didn't work. At first the person may have seemed to adjust his new approach, but, after a short time, the unwanted pattern of behavior returned.

Many experienced managers have concluded that it's a waste of time to try to change their people's performance. These managers have become worn down over the years trying to put corrections in. Why beat a dead horse? they think. Why engage in an exercise in futility?

But even these hardened veterans can learn how well this technique works in developing their people, creating a norm of learning, and adding needed capacity without adding additional costs. The MMOT process gives them a way to accomplish their instinctive desire to address these situations effectively over time and experience. These veterans will come to understand how to take direct charge of their managerial approach. They will go from skeptics to practitioners, and, as everyone knows, there's nothing like a convert.

The MMOT asks and answers these questions: *What happened? How and why did it happen? What can we learn that we will use next time?* and, finally, *How do we know that it's working?*

This technique follows a form, but it is not a formula. It is not a superficial set of prepackaged questions you ask, nor is it a questionnaire you fill out. The point of the form is to enable you and the person you are working with to better understand why the situation turned out as it did and what we can learn from that understanding.

The form is straightforward and easy to understand and apply. Its logic improves your chances of a successful learning and mentoring experience with your team.

The basic technique has four steps:

1. acknowledge the truth;
2. analyze how it got to be that way;
3. create an action plan;
4. establish a feedback system.

Each one of these steps is important. No step will work if the previous steps have not been completed. Each takes special skills, and each leads to the next.

STEP ONE: ACKNOWLEDGE THE TRUTH

Let's say that one of your direct reports misses an important due date. How can you make the most out of this situation?

The first step is to acknowledge the situation. Acknowledgment is not simply the act of you stating *your* point of view. It is important that the person you are working with recognizes reality too.

The point of step one is this: both you and the person understand that reality is what it is. In some ways this should be very simple to accomplish. But too often people mix the facts with how it got to be that way, and what it means, and who is to blame. When the conversation runs from one topic to another, it is hard to get a fix on a simple statement of facts.

One way we could describe the MMOT technique is as a "stay on topic" exploration. We need to be rigorous in each of the steps by staying on topic until we have accomplished the point of the step.

The point is that, together, both of you are on the same page about reality. When working with step one it is best to state reality as pure fact, rather than editorial.

"The data was due November 23, and now it's November 29."

State only the facts, not how this situation made you feel, or how the person let you down. Don't talk about how the situation got to be that way during this step in the process. That comes in step two.

Your job is to help the person acknowledge the facts. While this should seem simple enough, it is surprising how often people find it hard to acknowledge reality as it is.

Consider these examples of typical responses that do not acknowledge reality:

MANAGER
"The data was due November 23, and now it's November 29."
DIRECT REPORTS
"Well, there are lots of things that are behind too."
"I was swamped with other things."
"We had a Thanksgiving break."
"I was in Chicago."
"My kid just started college."
"I had trouble with my computer."
"I'm really sorry. It won't happen again."

Why do people find it hard to acknowledge the simple truth? They experience conflict. In their attempt to reduce feelings of conflict, they deflect away from reality. This is a natural reaction, but one that makes it harder for them to agree with the obvious. Their reaction drives them into a subjective frame of reference in which they focus on *how they feel*, rather than *what is true*. They want to get the heat off.

Here is where a good manager gets to show her stuff—by helping the person move from being subjective to being objective about reality. This is a simple but profound transformation.

Many of the replies listed above are motivated by this "get the heat off" dynamic. What is so hard about the fact that "*The data was due November 23, and now it's November 29*"? When we are being objective, nothing. When we are being subjective, we don't like how we feel about the facts, so we want to look away from the truth.

Often your job during an MMOT is to be a guide, leading the person through the initial subjective reaction, then helping him to see reality as it is, objectively. The movement through this territory is evolutionary, traveling from the starting point of an evasion of reality, to an acceptance of reality, to actively seeking reality, and finally to embracing reality.

When the MMOT becomes standard operating procedure for an organization, truth and reality are no longer seen as threats, but rather as powerful allies in reaching higher performance.

Agreeing with the facts

Knowing that people may first react to their discomfort by turning away from reality, you need to state the facts *and* make sure that the person *agrees* with the facts.

Even though you are leading the charge, this is not a one-way communication. It is important that you recognize whether or not the person has agreed with your description of reality. Often, you may think that the person has agreed, but he has only sidestepped a difficult conversation. It's as if he is saying, "Well, there's more to it than that, so give me a break." People usually aren't aware that they are motivated by their reaction to the conflict they feel, so their attempts to evade the facts are not made with malice aforethought. Rather this is an automatic reaction to the conflict they feel. Let's look at the assumptions that the responses listed above imply:

"Well, there are lots of things that are behind too" implies that while the due date was missed, you shouldn't be singling me out because others are just as guilty.

"I was swamped with other things."
"We had a Thanksgiving break."
"I was in Chicago."
"My kid just started college."
All imply that it was the circumstances that made it difficult for me to get the data in on time, and therefore you should have sympathy for my situation and not hold me accountable for this outcome.

"I had trouble with my computer" implies that circumstances beyond my control caused this to happen, and therefore it was not my fault.

"I'm really sorry. It won't happen again." While this may be a sincere apology, it may also imply that because the person feels badly about the situation, we need not address it. *"It won't happen again"* is often said to get the heat off rather than to "own" the situation.

As we have said, the goal of step one is to establish reality so you can build upon it. If you state the facts, you need to know that the person agrees with you in both the letter and the spirit of the truth.

"The data was due November 23, and now it's November 29. Is that right?"
"Yes."

This is a big "yes." It is a foundation upon which change of pattern, approach, thought, or outlook can be built.

Avoid subtext

Acknowledging reality is the act of stating reality truthfully and objectively. *Avoid derogatory subtext such as:*

"You let me down."
"You are incompetent."
"You are inept."
"You are not very professional."

Even if they might want to be open, the individuals who are on the receiving end may find it difficult not to feel defensive. They will most likely be taking the statement of reality very personally indeed. Even the most secure managers will tend to be reactive, especially if they have not experienced this technique before.

You need to define the context of the MMOT by your words and your tone. What it means, in this example, is that a result didn't come through on the promised time. This is the *only* message that the manager should deliver. It is as if you are saying, "Let's back up and take a look at reality together. Are you seeing what I'm seeing?"

A value conflict

To succeed at step one, you must tell the unvarnished truth. Sometimes truth and emotional comfort are in conflict. If avoiding emotional discomfort is the priority, a person will avoid the truth if it might provoke uncomfortable feelings.

On the other hand, when truth is the higher value, individuals may feel uncomfortable about reality, but they will still pursue an honest view of reality.

In professional life, establishing reality and truth is almost always more important than trying to avoid uncomfortable feelings. The consummate professional is one who can make things come out right, no matter what the circumstances. As we work through the MMOT, we are helping our people increase their state of professionalism, and each MMOT becomes a building block for greater professional development.

If you are successful in accomplishing step one, the person may lean toward acknowledging truth rather than avoiding discomfort. He may not even know that's what happened. But you will find that the person has a new interest in becoming fluent in reality. Why? Because, ironically, the more we face reality as it is, the less emotionally reactive we are to it. We become acclimatized to the truth. After a while, we will accept no substitutes.

Create truth telling as an organizational norm

We are creating a platform for truth. If truth were told only occasionally, the impact on the organization would be hit or miss. So for the MMOT to take hold, *truth telling must be an organizational norm.* But just saying it doesn't make that happen any more than listing value statements and putting them on the walls creates a culture that adheres to those values.

We need to teach our team that it's okay to tell the truth, even when the news is bad. As managers, we need to understand the starting point we all face: people are not used to being as candid as they need to be when the news is uncomfortable. That is the "before." The "after" is that people see it as part of their jobs to call it like it is, warts and all. We want to deliver the following message to the individuals and our team:

It's "safe" to tell the truth around here, but it's *not* okay *not* to tell the truth.

Once you begin naming reality accurately, people will feel uncomfortable at first, especially if you haven't in the past. But they will become used to it. Soon, people will get into the habit of telling each other the truth. This alone will improve performance.

STEP TWO: ANALYZE HOW IT GOT TO BE THAT WAY

One of your jobs in step two is to help your report think through the process that she used.

The question the two of you are addressing is "How are we to understand what happened?"

The spirit of this step is a real exploration of the decisions the manager made. What were the assumptions, and did they turn out to be true? What was the actual planning process?

You need to bring the person into a true process of analysis. We are not problem solving. We are not listing excuses. We are not inventing theories that are designed to explain facts we don't understand. Rather, *we are tracking the person's thought process.* We are learning together. What happened first, and then what happened? What decisions did you make? Why did you make those decisions? What was the outcome of those decisions?

Here's a sample exploration

"What happened that the due date was missed?"

"Well, I guess I just got too busy with all the things I've got to do."

"Is the date we put on this the right date? In other words, did we need to have your part done in this time frame?"

"Yeah, because Marketing needed the info for their ad campaign. So, yeah, that date was part of a larger project."

"Given that you needed to make the date, how did you think about it when you took on the assignment?"

"I didn't realize it would take as long as it did."

"Why not?"

"Well, I just didn't."

"Could you have known if you had done better planning?"

"In this case, yeah."

"Although you made an assumption about how long it would take, that assumption turned out not to be right. Is it safe to say you didn't think it through?"

"Yeah, I didn't. I assumed it wouldn't take too long. But, as it turned out—when I began to work on it, I suddenly was swamped with everything coming all at once—this and a number of other things."

"I see. When you thought about how you were going to do this project, did you add the other stuff you were also going to do to the equation?"

"No."

"What does that suggest?"

"To get the whole picture. To consider all the things I've got to do."

"Is that something you do from time to time: underestimate how long it will take to accomplish your goals and also not consider all the other things you've got to do?"

"Yeah."

"Okay, so one approach we can take is to have a better system to think through the demands of any project. If you had known this project would have been as involved as it turned out to be, what would you have done?"

"Started about two weeks sooner."

"Good, that's one idea. Now, sometimes it happens that you can't start sooner for some projects—you need information from someone else or you need a decision to be made and so on. If that were true in this case, what could you have done?"

"I could have moved some of my other work up, so it would have been done well before the other project hit."

"If you did that, would it have worked in this case?"

"Yes."

"What are you noticing about your work patterns?"

"I need to get a better fix on how much time it'll take to get a project done, and I have to factor in what's on my plate. I've got to create a more realistic schedule for myself."

"Good."

Performance

In helping a person analyze his performance, it is helpful to understand that there are two elements to consider. One is *design*, the other is *execution*.

Together good design and execution are the keys to first-rate performance. But too often one of these elements is missing.

The best design can be undermined by a lack of good execution. Think of a well-designed racing boat with a crew that does not do its job well. This group is unlikely to win the race.

Bad design works against good execution. People must work harder than they should because the design does not support their effort and may even work against them. Think of a great crew having to work against the inadequacies of a poorly designed racing boat. They will have trouble winning the race.

Bad design, along with bad execution, makes it hard to understand what is going on. Is it the design? Is it the people? The crew and boat have a good chance to end up in last place.

If we find that dates are missed because of poor design such as work-flow issues, process difficulties, or wrong sequencing, we can work to improve design.

The quality movement has taught us to focus on elements of business process design and to rethink our processes. This can lead to dramatic quality improvements. Sometimes the MMOT is less about execution than design.

"How did the date get missed, Ian?"

"I had to wait for Ralph to get the numbers for me."

"You couldn't do anything until you had the data?"

"Well, I suppose I could have worked around it and just plugged in the numbers when they came in."

"Would that have worked?"

"Yes. I didn't need the numbers to create the forms we needed. I could have used a placeholder. Ralph could only get the numbers to me after the 14th. So, I could have plugged them in around the 15th, and it would have been done on time."

In this example, the elements of design were time, sequence of events, the due date, and the date the numbers would be available.

In the above example, design is a very simple matter of sequencing two elements. But the order of events changes the possibility of success.

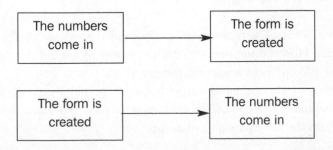

Sometimes a lackluster performance is a product of design, sometimes execution, sometimes both. In step two, you may need to explore both elements to truly understand how things turned out as they did.

Those elements of performance that fall into execution include:

Competence
Assumptions
Work habits
Ability to delegate
Follow-through with others
Decision making
Clarity of roles, rules, outcomes, current reality
Creativity
Flexibility
Steadfastness

Elements of performance that fall into design include:

Sequence
Scheduling
Accountability
Workload-capacity relationships
Built-in conflicts of interest
Contradictory or reinforcing reward systems
Delivery delays
Inventory availability
Work flows
Available technology

The point of step two is to understand the manager's thought process. How did the person make decisions? What did the person assume? Were these assumptions correct?

Often a walk through the story helps you to understand the critical decision points in the story. Here are typical types of questions that help track the sequence of events:

"When you got the assignment, how did you think about it?"

"Who was going to do what?"

"How did you think about the overall demands on your time?"

"Who was accountable for the various tasks?"

"When did you realize that you were off schedule?"

"What did you do about it?"

"How did you plan on getting the result accomplished on time and with the right level of quality?"

"When things didn't go the way you originally thought, what decisions did you make?"

"How did you track how well they worked?"

"Given the situation, how did you plan to change your approach?"

After you have tracked the story, you should have a clear idea of the events, the decisions that were made, the assumptions that need to be rethought, the impact of sequencing and scheduling, the repeatable patterns that lead to less-than-suitable outcomes, the impact of expectations with subcontractors and suppliers, and so on.

The job in step two is to understand what happened, not to assign the blame for faulty behavior. The key to step two is to reach a high level of understanding cause and effect through objective analysis. Clarity creates even more clarity.

STEP THREE: WALK AWAY WITH AN ACTION PLAN

Toward the end of working with the person, both of you will think about various ways to adjust the process. Unless we translate our insights into direct action, we will squander many of our discoveries. We need to craft an action plan, which may be very simple, such as: "From now on I'll check with Sue before I place the order." Or it may have many working parts. Whatever the level of complexity, it is important that it is written down clearly. We are making agreements, and we need to know exactly what we are agreeing to. This action plan will lead naturally to another moment of truth:

- The actions will or will not have been put into practice.
- The person will or will not begin to produce the desired results.

The new MMOT may be another adjustment to process, or it may be a simple "Well done."

The action plan should make sense, be practical and effective, be doable, and have a built-in feedback system so progress can be measured as the manager applies it to her work.

In the above example, the manager discovered he often didn't consider how long a project may take or consider the other projects in which he was involved. Here is how a plan for next time may be worked out:

"When's the next time you are accountable for a similar project?"

"I've just taken one on."

"When's the due date?"

"In five weeks."

"Given what we now know, what types of changes to your managerial process would you make?"

"The first thing is to get a more realistic fix on what it will take."

"How will you know you have a realistic assessment on what it will take?"

"Looking at the scope of the work, the resources I have—those kinds of things."

"That's good. What else?"

"Well, I don't want to be surprised, so I'd better take a look at my whole workload to see the demands on me. I'd better be a little more savvy about how I schedule what I do."

"If you took those steps, does it look likely you'll make your deadlines?"

"Yeah, it does."

In this example, the manager is helping the person to use the analysis of step two to form a plan. Since the person's blind spots are now apparent, the plan is very simple and obvious to create. Although not essential, it is better if the plan is invented by the person himself, but you cannot leave it up to the person alone. You must think the plan through yourself. Is it workable? Is it practical within the set of circumstances the person will face? Are the assumptions built into the plan sound?

The plan represents an intervention to a pattern. Does it look likely that this intervention will work if the person takes these steps? If the answer is yes, we're in good shape. But if the answer is no, there is more work to do.

When the person you are leading through an MMOT cannot conceive of a new approach to the work patterns you both discovered, you might suggest changes. While this is not as desirable as the person creating the plan herself, it still can enable good solid change. If you create the plan for her, will she understand it? Will she take it to heart? Will she make it work?

Often step two makes the person's blind spots so clear that new plans are easy to conceive. However, step two can be an adventure in making sure the subject of the MMOT is looking at reality objectively and not simply trying to get the heat off by casting herself in the role of victim of circumstances.

Yes, but . . .

Transactional analysis describes a game people play which is called "Yes, but . . ." One person presents a problem, and the other person suggests possible solutions. The next move in the game is the person with the problem pointing out the flaws in the solution. Another suggestion is offered, but the person finds flaws with this new idea, too. On it goes, until the second person gives up offering solutions. The game is over when the second person can announce, "See, there's nothing I can do about it."

In creating a plan, that last thing you want to do is become the unwitting partner in a game of "Yes, but . . ."

"You could try to schedule your work better to make sure you're spreading things out well."

"Yes, but I can't do that because I don't know when other assignments might come in."

"Well, you could call the people you are working with and see if they can give you a heads-up."

"Yes, but I can't do that because they get their assignments at the last minute."

"Well, figuring that there'll be some work coming in at the wrong time for you, you could write that into the system and try to plan accordingly."

"That's a great suggestion. The thing is, I'm too busy right now with what I'm doing to add anything to my already cramped load. No matter how much planning I try to do, it's going to get changed anyway."

And on it goes.

To go past this type of resistance you need to end the game.

"You know, every time I suggest something, you find some way it isn't going to work. Since that's the case, and since you need to find a better way to work this issue than you have, you'd better come up with a workable plan and make sure you put it into place and get it to work."

The last comment is an MMOT within an MMOT. It calls attention to the form the person is using and reminds the person that his accountability needs management. You are there to help figure out a way to get there, but it is not on your shoulders to "solve his problem." When one is accountable for an outcome or a process, it is up to him to see to it *personally* that the result is achieved. That is the meaning of accountability.

The workable plan

We have acknowledged reality, analyzed the process that led to this result, and calculated changes that look likely to work. From this insight, we can articulate a plan to use from this point on. This plan should be captured in writing by the subject of the MMOT himself.

"So, you are going to spend a little time seeing what this project will

take, and you're going to take a step back, look at your entire work sched-
ule, and be more realistic about your process, is that right?"

"Right."

"Good. Now can you send me an e-mail by Friday that summarizes
what we've said, the current pattern and the way we're going to address it,
so we both have a copy of this talk?"

"Okay."

This follow-up e-mail provides both of you with a record of what
has been said. Also it will give you a chance to see how well the person understands the content of the MMOT. You can correct the person's impression if it is somehow off the mark. This gives you
another chance to let the person know what you mean. It also gives
you a chance to express your resolve to ensure the situation improves.

The context of all of this is support for enhancing the person's
performance.

STEP FOUR: CREATE A FEEDBACK SYSTEM

Another common mistake that we make as managers is to pre-
sume that the talk we had was all we needed to do to put the correction in place. Too often, the correction needs further adjustment or
the manager needs additional support. The follow-up e-mail is a
good start, but we need more. We need a feedback system so we have
a chance to make adjustments in real time, as the person is putting
the plan into practice.

"We need a feedback system to track how things are going. Why don't
you drop by when you've figured out your schedule for the next project and
run it by me. That way I can support you in getting through this next
one."

"Okay."

"How about seeing me the first of next week? Is that enough time for
you to do your planning?"

"Yeah, that'll work."

In this example, only one meeting is scheduled. But it will probably take more meetings over the course of the five weeks to assure the plan is working well. They usually include a quick review of how things are going. Your suggestions can assure that the person will have a higher chance of success. Both of you are learning how to work together better. You are getting to know the strengths and weaknesses of the person, and therefore, you can add assistance as needed.

If we are successful, the MMOT will institute a change to the person's managerial process, and you will not need to hold his hand through their process again. While it takes a little time to work with him this way, your chances of improving his performance go up. It's unlikley that you will need to go over this same ground again.

It is easy to overlook the power of this final step. It is a permanent feature of great mentorship. As managers, we strive to get our associates to a strong level of performance and hope we can then turn our attention to our responsibilities. Yet, for a top-notch leader, there aren't "responsibilities" more important than continuous improvement in the excellence of our management team. Great basketball coaches aren't about the x's and o's. They are about the growing capacity of the team to execute from the chalkboard to the basketball floor, making the team the best it can be. Similarly, great leaders build capacity in their people every day by noticing what's working and what isn't, and offering immediate suggestions for improvement. The role particularly of executive leadership is achieving the objective of the organization through others. Enabling and encouraging others to generate superior results through improved management skills is the core of executive leadership, and providing effective feedback is our primary tool in the process.

Moreover, feedback isn't an event, it's a practice or what Aristotle calls a *habit*. In distinguishing between *dispositions* and *habits*, Aristotle argues, "*Habit* differs from *disposition* in being more lasting and firmly established." Indeed, for Aristotle, even moral virtues are habits precisely because, once established, they "cannot be easily displaced." Such "habits" are not superficial behavioral traits for Aristotle. They are the foundation of what is deep and abiding in how we conduct ourselves in the world.

Similarly, great leadership entails a deeply embedded, consistent approach to feedback. Like Aristotle's habits, giving feedback is a "firmly established" leadership practice. And just as it is possible to learn new habits in other areas of our lives, establishing the habit of providing feedback is foundational to a learning organization. A learning organization is committed to a norm of continuous feedback—openly and honestly supporting what's working, suggesting corrections for what isn't, and doing so in real time. Being open to giving and receiving immediate feedback, quickly addressing what needs to change, is an essential component of leadership that consistently turns out great performance.

More Than a Behavioral Change

The four steps create a complete form of the Managerial Moment of Truth technique. We know what happened, how it got to be that way, what we have learned so we can make changes to the approach next time, and how we will know how well the new plan is working.

But the learning is often more profound than simply a correction of a behavior. You are establishing a mentoring relationship with your team. The actions that speak louder than words say, "We can tell the truth and it will be okay. We can learn, and that is part of our job. We can improve professionally, and that is an aspect of our professionalism. We can change when we need to, and that is good. The organization has room for learning, and those things that are less than what they should be can be addressed effectively."

More than that, the MMOT sets up a fair game in which people succeed or fail based on the merits of their own efforts. With all the talk about empowerment in the last number of years, there are few things as powerful as truth that actually empowers the individual. No one can play fairly when politics is the centerpiece of management. No one can play fairly when mistakes go unaddressed. No one can play a fair game when the best performers are burdened with all the work while the others are ignored.

The MMOT is more than a technique. It is a way of life for the organization, one that is positive, hopeful, full of learning, and full of promise for the future. The product of the MMOT is people who are involved, consistently improving their performance over time, becoming more masterful at their respective professions. What could be better?

Now that we've introduced the four steps to the MMOT process, let's look at the common performance patterns we will encounter in our journey.

2
How to Recognize and Change Performance Patterns

As we have seen, the managerial moment of truth comes from two events: our awareness that there is a difference between the expected and actual performance, and our decision whether or not to address this discrepancy. If we choose to address it, what do we want to achieve?

The typical answer is to solve a performance problem.

Problem Solving

While many managers boast that they are professional problem solvers, there are many built-in drawbacks to a problem-oriented approach. When we engage in problem solving, our focus is on what we don't want—*the problem*. The actions we take are designed to have the unwanted problem go away.

If we solve the problem, we have absence of the problem. *But we may not have what we really want.* A problem-oriented management approach casts us in the role of getting rid of things, not in the role of creating the outcomes we want to create.

Since the managerial moment of truth usually begins with a performance problem, it is natural to think that what we are doing is discovering just what the problem is and then solving it.

Yes, we do want to change the faulty patterns of behavior. But we want so much more than that.

When we switch our attention from what we don't want to what we do want, we become very clear about the actual result we want from the MMOT intervention. Here are a few things we might want each person to be:

- exceptional in performance
- competent to do the job
- self-generating
- able to learn and improve
- a team player
- a valued member of the team
- a professional you can always count on
- a thought leader for the other team members

Perhaps this list is too ambitious. Or perhaps it is exactly the type of people we want around us. Too often we assume that we are stuck with who we have, and they can't change. Add to that the fact that we are exceedingly busy and we have our own accountabilities to manage. We need to make do with what we've got, so we concoct a process to get things done.

This modus operandi is designed to compensate for our team's inadequacies. Some of the key assumptions built into the compensation are:

- There's just so much time.
- People can't change, and even if they can, it takes too long to change them.
- Given my constraints, I've got to get the work done on time.

Some of these assumptions may be true, but not all of them. Let's take a look at each of them.

THERE'S JUST SO MUCH TIME

While the statement seems to be fact, it is how we *use* time that counts. Too often to the busy manager, time seems to pass in short, congested moments. There is a drum solo of activities: meeting after meeting, reports to write or review, projects to track, decisions to make. And with fewer layers of management in the modern organization, there are more and more direct reports to manage. No wonder we find ourselves focused on the immediate situation at hand within a short-term time frame.

The excessive short-term focus crowds out the time to conduct longer-term planning. While we would like to step back and reflect on how to better structure the process, that exercise seems like a luxury we just can't afford.

The question is: How long can we continue to stay in this short-term universe before we hit a brick wall? Many managers hit that wall years ago, and they live in a state of constant frustration, pressure, stress, feeling that there is no way out. Often, as the organization becomes more successful, more demands are put on the manager to do more with less. Things just get harder and harder as you try to meet your professional responsibilities.

The next question is: Can you afford *not* to take the time to build the capacity you need? More of the same will give you more of the same, which will simply make matters worse.

Yes, we are busy. Who isn't? And we can't wait for the "right" time when things slow down. They won't. That means we have to carve out time to plant seeds for the future.

If we can address the lackluster performance patterns of our managers and get them up to speed, we will have more capacity to use later on. Yes, it takes time to do that, but we need to find the time. If we do, things will get better.

Think of this as an investment, because that's exactly what an MMOT is. Think about the future state you want to build within your team. Think about the current situation you have now. And decide to take the time to move from the current situation to the future desired state.

PEOPLE CAN'T CHANGE, AND EVEN IF THEY CAN, IT TAKES TOO LONG TO CHANGE THEM

Here is a digital description of all the possibilities we all face:

- Your team can change.
- Your team can't change.

And if they can change:
- They can change in an acceptable amount of time.
- They can't change in an acceptable amount of time.

If left unaddressed, there's a good chance that your weaker performers will not change, improve their performance, grow, learn, or come up to speed.

How can we know who falls into the category of "can change adequately in an acceptable amount of time" when given a chance?

Often we don't. Often the people we have written off can come back to life through the MMOT process.

But taking the time to work with the weaker manager does involve a *risk* on your part—a risk that, as a strong performer, you may be hesitant to take. You've earned your "chops" by delivering on a standard of excellence, on time, and on budget. Putting the project in a less capable manager's hands—even with close supervision—may put your reputation in jeopardy. The project could slip, which would reflect badly on you. You have an apparent dilemma. Either you are going to build capacity in your novice managers or you (or someone else on your team) will be unduly burdened with their work. On deeper reflection, the apparent dilemma breaks down. It will never make sense to have weaker performers playing solitaire on their computers while you stay until 10:00 P.M. to get the product out. Either you contract with them to change their performance through techniques like MMOT or you need to replace them. Replacing people is more costly and never a surefire solution. So take the time to address their deficiencies and help them become great managers. While it may not work, it does give people a chance they would not have otherwise. And there is little that is more rewarding than watching a C player become an A player as the result of your coaching.

After working with a person using the MMOT technique, if it turns out that he is unable to change adequately in an acceptable amount of time, then both of you will know that there is a mismatch between the demands of the job and that person's capabilities. When that's the case, the manager's responsibility is to move the person out of that role. Using the MMOT ensures that those choices come out of a process that is fair, supportive, and clear. In our experience that's the story about 10 percent of the time. About 90 percent of the time the person can improve his performance to an acceptable level, and many often go well beyond that, all in an acceptable amount of time. The percentages may not be the same in your organization or on your team, but the most common experience of managers using the MMOT process is this: a higher percentage of people than they would have thought possible can and do become good players.

To tar everyone with the same "they can't change" brush is a distortion of reality. When the MMOT is built into the organizational process, people are given a chance to improve. In many ways, these people are given a new lease on their professional lives.

In truth, most people want to be more involved in the work of the organization. They want to play an important role, want to succeed, and are willing to do what it takes to become more accomplished.

The converse is also true. People do not like to be marginalized, having no place to go, having no way of playing a more important role. They feel frustrated, disappointed, and underutilized.

People are hungry to become more involved in their professional lives, but they usually don't know how to change their work patterns. It is hard for them to see their own patterns through their blind spots. That's why one of the most important mentoring relationships they have is with their manager. Through the MMOT, both employee and manager can go well beyond the current patterns and reach higher and higher levels of performance.

GIVEN MY CONSTRAINTS, I'VE GOT TO GET THE WORK DONE ON TIME

This assumption is undoubtedly true. Just remember, though, there will be work that must be done on time in the future too. If we let the immediate demands run us ragged, the future workload-capacity relationship is only going to be more of the same or even worse. Part of our job is to develop our people because, when we do, we are adding capacity to our shop.

We always work under constraints. The question is, Can we change the nature of the constraints? Often the constraints people experience have to do with trying to accomplish more under the same set of conditions. The MMOT approach enables you to change the conditions so that you have fewer constraints over time.

One constraint is the capacity of your best players. When you load the work on them, they feel more and more pressure. They know that they are taking on the lion's share of the work. They feel it is unfair. They can't understand why you don't manage the situation better. Over time, your leadership comes into question, and your best players burn out.

Top performers' burnout is only one challenge in how MMOT affects them. As leaders we savor our best performers. They consistently deliver day in and day out with little attention. However, what happens when they do need attention? Our first instinct is to let it go. After all, 95 percent of the time their work is excellent. But if their performance is less than acceptable, it could become more common until someone you have consistently counted on becomes less reliable. Even if you recognize this as a growing problem, the logic of applying MMOT rigorously may not seem obvious. After all, this person is a good, often great employee. He can get a job across the street, and probably for more money. The last thing we want to do is demotivate him or have him feel he is being overmanaged. He probably recognizes that, relative to others, he is still more than carrying his weight.

Unfortunately, there is no way out if you aspire to a culture of truth telling. *Naming inadequate performance and monitoring it for improvement demands consistent application if we want it to transform a culture.* When we universally apply MMOT to all situations that demand it, everyone gets the same message—candor trumps concern about offending top performers or anyone else; it represents the organization's resolve to be great. Another thing that happens is that top performers are often their own worst critics, so they are likely already coming down on themselves for their performance. But they often won't know how to self-correct. Great athletes like Tiger Woods, the Williams sisters, Andre Agassi, and Michael Jordan have had slumps in their careers. And in each case they went to their coaches for improvement. They look at films of themselves and then go back out and practice, practice, practice. It isn't much different for top-tier management. What may have worked with one team may not be working now, and as a professional, I want to know what to change and how to change. MMOT used appropriately doesn't put your top performers at risk; it brings them closer to an organization that demands universal commitment to candor and improved management.

Real and Lasting Change

Most managers have tried to change the performance of their less-accomplished people. The usual pattern they have experienced is this: a temporary improvement in performance, followed by a plateau, followed by a regression to the original unacceptable situation. This is an oscillating pattern in which movement forward is reversed. If your experience has been a series of oscillating patterns, it would be natural to give up trying to improve your team.

There are reasons oscillating patterns exist. The most common has to do with motivation.

REACTING TO CONFLICT

One of the oldest motivations in history is trying to get people to change their ways by reacting to *conflict*. The first step in the pattern is a sense of conflict. The second step is taking corrective action evoked by the conflict.

We feel pressure to get our car inspected on time or to file our tax form before April 15, and we force ourselves into action by thinking about the bad things that will happen to us if we don't get them done. When the situation is short term, it can seem to work. But if we are talking about long-term change, this structure leads to an oscillating pattern. Here's what happens over a more extended time:

Conflict drives action designed to reduce the conflict. Once the action is taken, the conflict is reduced, even if the situation hasn't changed. You see a news item on CNN about the diabetes epidemic, and you decide to reduce your intake of carbs. After about a week, you feel better about it all. You are no longer experiencing the conflict you had. The next thing you know, you are eating exactly the same diet you had before you saw the program on diabetes. This pattern always leads you back to the situation you were trying to change.

Here's another description of the pattern: more conflict leads to more action, which leads to less conflict, which leads to less motivation to continue the corrective action we took at first, and therefore, a regression to the original behavior.

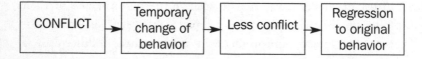

This structure is self-defeating. Even if your suggestions are useful and well intentioned, the person is simply reacting to the conflict he feels, and you can expect temporary improvement followed by a return to the old work patterns.

You have called a meeting with one of your direct reports. You begin to point out that the performance of one of his managers is still substandard. During your last meeting your direct report agreed to manage a 5 percent cost reduction. Not only did the cost not go down, it has gone up an additional 2 percent. Your direct report is embarrassed and disappointed at not having accomplished what he agreed to. The conflict he feels, rather than the outcome you both want, becomes the underlying motivation for his next actions.

Too often well-meaning managers unintentionally set an oscillating pattern into motion. The result will always be the same, temporary change and a regression to the original behavior. That's how the physics of it works.

"THE SKY IS FALLING" MANAGER

We all recognize this person, the one who manages through conflict. This person uses scare tactics to try to mobilize the troops through proclamations of crisis and visions of disaster. At first it seems to work. People roll up their sleeves and work extra hard. But next thing the team knows, it's another crisis. Over time, the team begins to ignore the manager's hysteria. Then the manager must increase the sense of crisis simply to get the same amount of work done. Unless the sky is really falling, shouting "the sky is falling" loses its impact fairly quickly.

This type of manager can't build capacity. Managing through conflict can only make people defensive, reactive, and subjective—not thoughtful, reflective, or objective. It cannot lead to a platform for truth because the conflict is based on distortion.

In reality there are times of real crisis that we must address. But if we are living with one proclaimed crisis after another, we know something's wrong in the planning process.

EMOTIONAL CONFLICT

We can understand that when we conduct an MMOT, the other person might be experiencing emotional conflict. That comes with the territory. How can we help people move from an oscillating reaction to real learning and improvement?

One thing that will help is to be clear about *our* motivation. What is the outcome we want to achieve? What is our goal?

When we move away from the problem-oriented frame and enter into an outcome-oriented frame, the goal becomes obvious: *we want great performers turning in great performances.* This goal is the centerpiece of our process.

When we are conducting an MMOT we should have that outcome clearly fixed in our minds. Even as we go through the four steps in the MMOT process, we need to be aware of our aim, which is to bring out the best in this person.

Here are two pictures of how the MMOT will play itself out over time:

- Short term: Reacting to the emotional conflict she feels, the person will adopt new behaviors motivated by her desire to reduce the conflict.
- Longer term: The person will realize that you are actually helping her to become more accomplished and that the MMOT is a vital mentoring experience that is a catalyst for professional development.

Unless we are motivated to create the outcome we want, rather than simply address the faulty behavior, the chance of the person changing her orientation doesn't change from short-term reaction to conflict to a focus on learning, developing great skills, and becoming a more accomplished manager.

PAST EXPERIENCES

One reason that managers ignore a moment of truth is that their past experience has not led to any real and lasting improvement, only to an oscillating pattern in which performance returns to what it was as soon as the heat's off. Another reason is that they dislike conflict and want to avoid it. In order to avoid feeling their own conflict, managers avoid the confrontation they anticipate.

As we saw in chapter 1, this is a conflict of values. Which one is more important to you: telling your team the truth or avoiding your own discomfort? Instead of understanding that they are dealing with a value conflict, many managers try to stay on the fence between these two often competing values.

When the situation renders these values mutually exclusive, it is hard to stay off the fence. This leads to another type of oscillating pattern in which you decide to address the situation but soften your approach in such a way that the person doesn't get the point. Knowing the outcome you are trying to create, which is *building more ca-pacity within your organization and bringing your team up to higher per-formance levels*, establishes truth as a higher value than avoiding discomfort.

The Overall Strategy

The overall strategy is this: to put in corrections early, before there is a need for a full-blown confrontation. This is not always pos-sible, of course. We need to deal with the reality we have, which is a result of how we dealt with moments of truth in the past. There may be some major adjustments the MMOT needs to address. There are always minor adjustments that can be made. By dealing with them you are planting the seeds for a future harvest.

As we have said, usually busy managers like to overlook minor deficits in performance. After all, they have more important things to do, and the discrepancy between the standard they wanted and the actual product is not big enough to mention.

Since it is not mentioned, the quality of work must be fine. At least that's the conclusion the person who did the work makes from the fact that it was accepted without comment. A managerial mo-ment of truth has come and gone, and the message inadvertently de-livered was "This work is fine."

If you begin to address the *minor* discrepancies between the de-sired standards and the actual standards, the MMOT technique is quick and easy to use. Little MMOTs, early on, can lead to dramatic improvement in how people work. The person can easily understand and adopt the adjustments. The person is not feeling as much con-flict as she might if the situation were of a greater magnitude.

If we see the MMOT technique as a training approach, we can develop our team's performance steadily. When reality is put on the table and people can tell each other the truth, they have the ability to make the needed adjustments. Moreover, they begin to use those moments when things are off course to adjust their process. They begin to actively evaluate their performance more perceptively. They begin to think in terms of how to better their own performance. They begin to feel professional momentum because they have a clear sense of a destination—higher performance levels.

It's not unusual for a person's professional evaluations to be filled with glowing report after glowing report, but then, suddenly, he receives a negative evaluation. Did the person suddenly change? Usually not. His performance has been consistent throughout all of those evaluations. It's not uncommon for people to be surprised by what seems to them a change in how they are perceived by their boss.

> *"Gee, I was doing fine, wasn't I?"*
> *"Well, I mentioned to you two months ago I was concerned about a couple of your projects not being on time."*
> *"I guess you did, but look at all the other stuff I've accomplished since then."*
> *"Look, I told you where you stood."*
> *"Actually, you didn't make it that clear. And you certainly didn't suggest it was going to have this kind of impact on my review."*

When we see such a pattern, we know that there has been a breakdown in truth telling. The person has not had accurate feedback to make needed adjustments. How can people know the standard we want if we don't tell them? How can we expect them to improve if we don't give them accurate and truthful feedback?

At first, the boss may think that the behavior will correct itself. But without truthful feedback, it doesn't. And then, like water torture, one drip after another after another, the boss finds that she can't stand it any longer. What seemed minor before is now a major issue.

Had the boss been truthful from the start, people would know where they stood. From their point of view, they have turned in acceptable work for a long time, and the new criticism seems unfair. Then there is a breakdown of the relationship between the manager and the direct report, making it harder for the manager to assume a mentor role.

The MMOT requires consistency of truth telling. Just like learning to play a musical instrument or playing a sport, adjustments need to be made regularly until the person masters the approach.

Mentorship

Managers often think, Look, I've hired these people and we pay them well. Why don't they just do their job like they're supposed to do? This is a fair question. But it is also a naive question in that it doesn't take reality into account. Even the most accomplished professionals need direction. For all of us, there are events that don't go right. It is helpful to use these events as learning experiences. It is also helpful to be in a collaborative process rather than having to go it alone. It is helpful when there is someone in the organization who supports us in bringing out our best.

No one is so self-sufficient that she does not need support and direction. Sometimes she needs clarity of goals, roles, norms, rules, and guiding principles. Sometimes she confronts situations in which her aspirations far outpace her current abilities, so she needs to develop her capabilities. Sometimes she needs to see a model of how one can carry oneself, or how one can think through a situation, or how a leader can engage others in a collective process. Sometimes she needs to hear "well done" when her performance has been exceptional.

While the term *mentor* has been around organizations for years, most people think that a mentor relationship is between an older, more experienced person and a few young Turks who are members of "the most likely to succeed" club. In many organizations, the superstars have mentors and everybody else is on their own.

A broader and more useful understanding of the mentor role is this: anyone can be a mentor for anyone else. People can learn from those who have more experience, of course. But they can also learn from people who have less experience, and therefore can ask new questions that don't build in previous assumptions. People can learn by looking up, down, and laterally in the organization.

All professionals are in the learning business. If you read the biog-
raphies of the most accomplished people in history, you'll learn that
they were always in a learning mode. Even when one reaches mastery in a field, there is always something new to learn, consider, and
think through.

More than ever, changes in the organizational landscape are moving with breathtaking speed. What we once knew and relied upon
may no longer be true or relevant. The old modality of mastering a
profession and then basing your life's work on your expertise is long
gone. Global economic migrations, revolutions in technology, trans-
formations in the foundation of markets, and a host of unexpected
developments repeatedly hit organizational life and overhaul all of
the rules. Learning has become one of the most critical competitive
advantages an organization can enjoy.

But learning is not an abstract platitude. Nor does it happen simply by an organization's declaring itself to be a learning organization.
It happens by the *fact* that *people are learning*, on both the individual
level and the collective organizational level.

If your organization is to accomplish its mission, your role as
mentor within the overall organizational learning process is vital.
Within Blue Shield of California, mentorship is a leadership principle. The leader must function as a mentor as part of her role. Blue
Shield is not alone in understanding the wisdom of this principle.

Great leaders are also great mentors. Greatness is hard to achieve
without a substantial amount of learning built into the fabric of the
organization. Mentorship is the most direct path to learning because
it is done within the context of real work set against the realities of
the world. Therefore, it is practical, relevant, immediate, important,
and straightforward—all the things the MMOT technique drives.

Patterns of Performance

When we back up and take a longer look at performance, we can
begin to see consistent patterns in play. As a mentor, you can open a
mother lode of insight when you study these patterns. You can help

your team learn from both the successful patterns and the less-than-successful patterns.

There are two tests for pattern recognition: *predictability* and *the ability to intervene and change the pattern.*

If we recognize a pattern, we can predict what is likely to happen in the future if nothing has changed. People are surprisingly true to their patterns. We tend to approach situations in typical rather than in atypical ways.

Our ability to perceive these patterns explains why we may give the more critically important work to our best performers, though, as we've said, this burns them out and fails to develop others.

We can become even more perceptive when we use the MMOT technique because the process helps us study patterns of decisions, assumptions, and actions. After we understand the dynamics that led to the outcome we are addressing, we then engage in a process of "pattern interruption." In step three a new plan is created, and in step four it is managed with the goal of setting a new pattern in motion.

Faulty performance is either chronic or an anomaly. It's a one-time deal or it is the modus operandi. In both cases, there is learning potential to explore. We can help change chronic patterns of faulty performance to chronic patterns of good performance. We can also learn general principles from the anomalies. As we use the MMOT with our people, the patterns change, becoming more successful. Over time, we train our people to be highly professional, capable, and strong learners and performers.

3

Case Study:
Working with a Team

The MMOT technique is as effective with teams as it is with individuals.

The following is an actual MMOT that was conducted by Trish, a Blue Shield of California manager working with one of her teams. Trish, a very astute manager, conducted this session soon after her very first exposure to the MMOT technique.

She was in the middle of a weekly meeting when she learned that the team had missed a due date. She used the MMOT to help the team understand its pattern and change it.

The team members were Frank and Jan from Marketing and John and Carl from Sales. The following is Trish's reconstruction of the occasion.

TRISH
"Okay, today is our due date for the marketing materials. So where are we?"

The team members suddenly looked down, averting their eyes from Trish, while others glanced nervously at one another. There were a few uncomfortable moments of silence until she finally said:

"Anyone?"

FRANK
"Well . . . [pause] We're a little late."

TRISH

"Oh? How late?"

JAN

"We're off by three days."

TRISH

"How come?"

FRANK

"We weren't able to get a full review of the materials by all the stake-holders."

TRISH

"We weren't?"

FRANK

"Not really."

TRISH

"We said we'd have it done by the due date—today."

JAN

"Things happen."

TRISH

"If we commit to a due date, we need to make it. There are people depending on us."

FRANK

"Yes, but sometimes it's hard to get everyone to send back their comments on time."

TRISH

"We're talking about reviewing materials, reading them."

FRANK

"I can't force people to get back to me."

Trish realized that she had not established step one in the process—to acknowledge reality—so she went back to that step.

STEP ONE: ACKNOWLEDGE REALITY

TRISH

"Okay, wait—wait. Before we get into how it happened, do we all agree that we said we'd have the marketing materials in by today and we are now three days behind?"

FRANK

"We were really trying to manage this thing."

TRISH

"I just want to make sure we're all on the same page about reality. Do we agree that today is the due date?"

"Yeah—sure—"

TEAM

TRISH

"Do we agree we are three days behind?"

JAN

"Yes."

TRISH

"So we all agree?"

TEAM

"Yes—okay."

At first, Frank was ready to talk about how hard he had tried to make the date. But Trish knows that she needs to make sure the building block—acknowledging reality—is in place, so she makes sure that everyone agrees with the fact that today is the due date and the team recognizes that they are three days behind schedule. Notice that the team is ready to drift from topic to topic. This is common with most teams. But Trish manages the team's focus carefully, insisting that everyone stay on topic

STEP TWO: ANALYZE HOW IT GOT TO BE THAT WAY

TRISH

"Good. So let's find out how we managed to be in this situation. And before we start, I want us to look at this thing together, objectively. Let's understand how we thought about this, what assumptions we made, what were the dynamics. Okay?"

TEAM

"Yup. Sure."

Trish establishes the focus clearly so that everyone knows what she is doing. Look at the words she uses: "find out," "look at this thing together," "objectively," "understand," "assumptions," "dynamics." She is helping her team know what they should be exploring. She is acting as a guide through the thought process. She makes sure that everyone understands the exercise before she begins to explore step two.

TRISH

"Now, Frank, you said that it took the stakeholders longer than expected. What stakeholders took longer?"

FRANK

"Some of the Sales folks."

TRISH

"Okay. Is that right, Sales people?"

CARL

"I didn't realize we had to review it."

FRANK

"I sent you an e-mail."

CARL

"I didn't get it."

FRANK

"Why not?"

CARL

"I was on the road and couldn't get my e-mail."

FRANK

"Well you should have—"

TRISH

"Wait a minute. Right now we're analyzing how it happened. Once we understand that, we'll talk about what to do next time."

Trish sees that the group is getting anxious, but she is not letting the team fall into a blame game. She realizes that Frank is implying that he would have made the date had Carl done his part. Carl is playing "victim of circumstances." Maybe Frank is right, that he is late because of Carl. Maybe Carl *is* a victim of circumstances. No good will come out of these guys arguing the toss. Trish puts them back on track so a real analysis can occur.

> TRISH
>
> *"Remember, we're just trying to understand what happened so we can learn from this and do a better job next time. So, you sent an e-mail, Frank?"*
>
> FRANK
>
> *"Right."*
>
> TRISH
>
> *"And you didn't get it?"*
>
> CARL
>
> *"Yeah. Well, I got it when I got back, but that was too late."*
>
> TRISH
>
> *"Did you know that Carl didn't get it, Frank?"*
>
> FRANK
>
> *"Not until now."*
>
> TRISH
>
> *"So, from your point of view, you had let Carl know, but in reality he didn't actually know because he was off e-mail. Is that accurate?"*
>
> FRANK
>
> *"Yes."*

Notice how beautifully Trish objectively tracks the events. She mastered both Frank's and Carl's viewpoints and tells them how it is from each of their individual points of view. She then makes sure that she has described reality accurately by checking with both Frank and Carl. Their agreement helps change the dynamic in the room. They are being guided to a more objective vantage point where they can begin to see the actual dynamics. The less defensive they are, the more they will be able to see and understand.

> TRISH
>
> *"Okay. Is that a pattern?"*
>
> JOHN
>
> *"Yeah. When we're on the road, it's hard to get our e-mail with any consistency."*

CARL

"Some places have it, some don't."

TRISH

"Marketing folks, did you know that?"

JAN

"No, not really."

Trish helps the Marketing folks see a factor that may have contributed to the late due date. Finding out that the Sales folks are sometimes off e-mail and that the Marketing folks didn't happen to know that helps advance the analysis. In the next few questions Trish tracks Sales's and Marketing's actual accountability in making the due date. Trish continues to guide her team to an objective analysis of reality.

TRISH

"Sales folks, even though you have trouble getting your e-mail on the road, did you know we had a due date for this marketing material?"

CARL

"Yes."

TRISH

"And you guys know we can't send it out without your okay?"

FRANK

"Well, we can."

JAN

"Yeah, but when we do, all we ever hear is that we should have run it by Sales."

TRISH

"I just want to make sure we're still on track here. Everyone knew we had today as the due date, right?"

TEAM

"Right."

TRISH

"And, Marketing, you were accountable for getting the result by today, right?"

FRANK

"Right."

TRISH

"And, Carl, you knew that these guys had today as the due date?"

CARL

"Well, yeah, I knew—but I got busy."

TRISH

"Were you accountable to get back to Marketing?"

CARL

"Yes."

TRISH

"What does 'busy' have to do with it?"

CARL

"Nothing."

Notice how the team drifts back into a defensive posture. Trish realizes the team is veering off track, and she brings them back by returning to step one—acknowledge reality. Reality is: Sales knew the due date was today but didn't manage their affairs accordingly. Carl implies that having the excuse of "being busy" somehow reduces his accountability. Many managers would give Carl a one-way speech about his accountability at that point. Instead, Trish continues to track Carl's thought process to the point where he sees that his assumptions about circumstances are not true. Through her questions, Trish has more access to Carl's assumptions and the subsequent decisions he made, and therefore a better chance to enable him to see reality.

Trish goes back to step one when she establishes that Marketing is accountable for the result. The interesting dialogue between Frank and Jan tells the story of a source of frustration for Marketing. Frank is being literal about his ability to send out marketing materials without the approval of the Sales folks. Jan complains that if they do that, they are admonished. Trish could follow this path, but instead she wisely reestablishes step one. Sometimes we need to revisit a previous step in the process if it seems to have gotten lost. Trish is moving the session ahead, but she restates anything that needs to be further acknowledged. She also sets up the team for the next step in the process: create a plan.

TRISH

"So we need to look at two things: how we got here and what we will do next time. As far as I can tell, we got here because you folks in Marketing relied on Sales to get back to you on time. And Sales, because you didn't have access to e-mail, even though you knew the due date and knew you needed to sign off on this material, you didn't make it happen. Is that a fair description of reality?"

TEAM

"Yes."

STEP THREE: CREATE A PLAN

TRISH

"Okay. Next step. What are we learning?"

FRANK

"That we have to take a more active role in managing the Sales folks."

TRISH

"Okay. What does that mean?"

FRANK

"I sent Carl an e-mail, but I didn't check to see if he got it. I didn't follow through. So I need to make sure we are clear with each other."

CARL

"And I could have looked at the calendar and have seen I needed to get the material back to you on time, Frank."

TRISH

"Marketing can make sure Sales understands what it's asked for, and Sales can do a better job with self-management?"

TEAM

"Yes."

TRISH

"Good. What else?"

JAN

"Well, we could publish a schedule so that everyone knows the timeline better. I mean, not just the due dates but when we need to have a final draft, when we need to proof it, when we need to add the graphics, when we need to get it to the printer."

CARL

"That would help."

JOHN

"Yeah."

Trish understands the ideas and explores them by putting them to the test: how will this plan play out given the situation the team described?

TRISH

"What about you Sales folks? You're on the road. You can't always get your e-mail. You're busy doing sales calls. You're not in the office. What can you do to stay in the loop?"

JOHN

"Simple. We can call in when there's a deadline and make sure we're on track."

FRANK

"That would help because it's hard to chase you guys down."

The team is beginning to work with each other collaboratively. Trish summarizes the insights and ideas the team has so far.

TRISH

"So here's where we are. We are three days late because of the way we've managed this thing. We have learned that there was some miscommunication, some folks letting circumstances get in the way of their accountability, and people from both Sales and Marketing making assumptions that weren't accurate. Is that right?"

TEAM

"Yes."

TRISH

"Now that we know that, we are going to do a number of things to make our deadlines, and to have Sales involved with the marketing material. First, we'll all agree about the due date. But that's not enough because this time we did all agree, but still we didn't make it. So while we

need to know the due date, we need to do more. Marketing is going to pub-
lish a schedule of the major events so everyone knows what's happening.
And Sales is going to make a point of contacting Marketing when they are
on the road and not getting their e-mail. Is that it?"

TEAM

"Yes."

Trish tests the plan again and pushes the team's thinking.

TRISH

"So, Frank, what happens if sales doesn't get back to you on time?"

FRANK

"We're going ahead. They had their chance, and if they pass their due
date, we go ahead anyway. So they need to comment on time or forever
hold their peace."

TRISH

"Sales, any questions? Does that seem fair to you?"

CARL

"Yup."

Sales and Marketing have just agreed on a plan that would exclude
Sales from the process if they miss their date. Trish takes a stand for
the company and refuses to have the circumstances determine the
best outcome.

TRISH

"Well, it's not fair to the company, because we need Sales involved with
this. Okay, so we have a fallback position. I want us to manage this process
so we have the best result in terms of quality as well as manage our due
date. That means we need Sales to review the materials."

CARL

"Right."

STEP THREE, CONTINUED

TRISH

"So when's the next time we are going to make a Marketing piece?"

JAN

"We need one first of next month."

TRISH

"Let's work that one through. How are we going to do it?"

JAN

"I'm accountable for this one."

TRISH

"Okay."

JAN

"I'm going to publish a schedule by, let's say, [looks at calendar] next Friday."

TRISH

"Okay."

CARL

"And who can we call when we're on the road?"

JAN

"Does anyone want to coordinate this?"

FRANK

"I'll do it."

TRISH

"Okay. What other thoughts are you having? Anyone?"

JAN

"We as a group need to evaluate how we do this next one."

CARL

"We need to understand what assumptions we're making, and if what we thought was true turns out to be true or not."

JOHN

"I think we've all been too passive. We need to drive this thing and not let it drift away."

JAN

"I feel better about next time."

CARL

"So do I."

STEP FOUR: ESTABLISH A FEEDBACK SYSTEM

TRISH

"Okay, let's create a feedback system so we know how well we're doing with these changes. Jan, how about you and I working together on this since you are driving this next one?"

JAN

"Sure."

TRISH

"Let's meet early next week, and we can talk about how the schedule works and how we can manage it."

JAN

"Sounds good. How about Tuesday?"

TRISH [CHECKS HER SCHEDULE]

"Ten-thirty, after the staff meeting?"

JAN

"Right."

This meeting led to a change in the team's performance. Sales and Marketing began to collaborate more closely, and the miscommunications virtually stopped. The team learned many lessons from that first MMOT. The members began to evaluate their performance with each major project, and they became one of the most effective and reliable teams in their division.

4

Developing Specific Skills

Each of the four steps in the MMOT technique requires specific skills. Many of these skills will be intuitive. Some of them are counterintuitive. All of them can help us become more effective with our people.

As we have seen, the MMOT is a mindful thought process, a dynamic exploration, a creative exercise in process planning.

There is also a leadership component in which we set the standards of excellence, understand the relationship of the details to the whole, and help our people build alignment and esprit de corps. The challenge is to find just the right way to bring out the best in individuals who have different personalities, different approaches to life, different rhythms and patterns.

No one MMOT is exactly like the next. Each time we engage in an MMOT, we are improvising within a logical form. We don't know how our questions will be answered. We don't know how the person or team will react. We must stay tuned throughout the entire process.

The Overall Desired Outcome

One prerequisite that needs to be in place is this: clarity about the outcome we are working to achieve. What do we want? As we have noted in chapter 2, we want exceptional performance from exceptional performers.

While this description is true, it is too broad and general to be terribly useful. For each member of your team, you need to have an outcome in mind that deals with two factors: the specific demands of the role he is playing and the type of member you want on your team and in the organization.

These two factors are the same as they are for various team sports, such as baseball. In baseball there is a demand for overall athletic competence and specific skills for each of the positions. The catcher plays a vastly different role than does the pitcher. Both of them, together, are a team within a team. They must create and implement their strategy against each hitter. The first baseman plays a different role than does the shortstop than does the right fielder. Many of these athletes can play each other's positions. But when any of them plays first base, he functions as a first baseman. When he plays outfield, he functions as an outfielder.

Within the organization there are the "players" and the positions. There needs to be a match between the talents and abilities of the player and the position. Sometimes a very talented professional doesn't know the function of the position, even though he may have the ability to play it well. In that case, the outcome we want is for this person to learn to play that position. Sometimes the person does not have all the skills needed to play a particular role. She may or may not be able to acquire them within an acceptable time frame. If not, there is a mismatch, and other arrangements need to be made. If she can, then the outcome we want for this person is to come up to speed quickly.

Consider the professional outcome you want for each person you manage. This is not the same as listing the deliverables you expect from these people. You are taking into account a wider spectrum that includes their abilities, skills, leadership competence, and ability to align with the team and the enterprise.

Each person plays a role, and you want to have a clear picture of the specific competencies required of each position. Each person has potential that can be developed. Have a clear idea of that potential, and what the outcome would look like when that person achieves that potential.

Your vision may include the team's ability to be self-generating and may include how it performs within larger teams—how the members work on their own and how they work with others.

Your vision may not be the same as theirs. Often we can see the potential in others more easily than they can see it in themselves. Once they have support, people often want to develop their professional potential and welcome the chance to grow.

A managerial moment of truth is about a specific event such as a missed date or critical mistakes, but it occurs within a broader context: your vision of this person's potential and the current level of performance, which is the actual manifestation of his potential. We not only address the particular performance issue; we also are working toward helping the person become more accomplished.

When we engage in an MMOT, we have the desired state in mind, even as we focus on the current conditions. Our term for this is *structural tension*.

The Principle of Structural Tension

When we work with our teams, we want to focus on two critical data points: the desired state and the actual state. This is the principle of structural tension.

Structural tension is used extensively in many successful organizations as a planning and management tool. And it is also useful within the MMOT process. We are clear about the outcome we want for the people we are supporting through the MMOT process, and we explore their actual performance so that we can become clear about current reality.

A WORD ABOUT THE TENSION-RESOLUTION SYSTEM

Whenever we establish a tension of any kind, it will seek resolution. Usually when people hear the word *tension*, they think about psychological stress, anxiety, and emotional conflict. The type of tension we are talking about has nothing to do with emotional states. Instead, it is structural, in that the tension is formed by the discrepancy between two related elements that are connected. Examples of this type of tension are found everywhere in nature, from simple to complex systems. Hunger, one of our most basic instincts, is a form of structural tension. The amount of food the body wants is different from the amount of food the body has. That is the dynamic in play. We eat to resolve this tension. The tension is resolved when the actual and desired amounts of food are the same.

In organizational life we use this dynamic to organize our management systems. To do this, we must be clear about our desired state—our goals, deliverables, strategic objects, and so on—and our current state in relationship to these outcomes. In the beginning of our managerial process, there will always be a difference between the full realization of our goals and our current circumstances. We can consciously manage structural tension by continuing to focus on our goals while making sure we understand where we are at any moment in current reality.

Sometimes people think that there is a "gap" between the desired outcome and current reality. A gap is the absence of something. Tension is the presence of a powerful dynamic that drives movement forward. If we were near a piano, we could demonstrate this point by playing a musical tension (such as a tritone, for those of you who know music). Dissonance would fill the air. The sound would lead to a natural resolution of the tension (a major chord), which we would clearly hear and understand. Contrast that with a gap. We wouldn't play anything at all. The room would be silent.

When we form structural tension, we are like an archer pulling back a bowstring and aiming an arrow at a target. An archer is working with natural structural forces, as should the manager. A vision of the outcome is only one element in the structure. The other is a clear understanding of reality. Together the two establish structural tension.

The tension can be resolved in one of two ways: give the desired outcome or accomplish the outcome. The resolution we want is that our desired state and the current state are the same—in other words, we resolve the tension by creating the outcomes we want.

The MMOT process establishes structural tension by positioning the current state of performance *against* the desired state. Throughout the process, we become clearer about both factors.

The Managerial Moment of Truth is based on structural tension by virtue of the contrast between the expected result and the actual result.

The first step in the MMOT technique is to acknowledge reality in relationship to the desired outcome: "The report was due on Tuesday and it's now Thursday." We are viewing reality in relationship to our desired outcome. When we are sufficiently clear, structural tension is adequate to propel us to our goal. In other words, there is more energy and motivation to bring the current state up to the level of the desired state.

Be clear about the outcome you want, both from the situation and more generally for your direct report. Be clear about the current reality in relationship to your desired outcome.

Events That Lead to MMOT

Here is a list of the most common situations in which we would use a corrective MMOT:

- expectations not met
- missed due dates
- unacceptable quality
- unclear or wrong goals
- wrong processes (too costly, too inefficient, et cetera)
- wrong values
- wrong strategy or tactics
- wrong attitude
- wrong orientation, spirit, et cetera
- wrong prep
- wrong information, data

STEP ONE SKILLS: ACKNOWLEDGING REALITY

There is more to acknowledging reality than meets the eye. Here are some skills that will enable you to help others see reality accurately and objectively.

Separate how it is from how it got to be that way.

It is natural to jump from topic to topic. It takes discipline to stay on topic. But if our people are to learn to acknowledge reality more easily, we must not let them change the subject. We will analyze how the situation got to be the way it is in step two of the MMOT process. In step three we'll talk about what to do about it. In step one we are simply stating the facts—*this is what reality is.*

Without establishing reality clearly, we would find it hard to move to the next steps. So we need to pay special attention to the facts as they really are.

It is not enough for us to assert the facts. The word *acknowledgment* in this sense means that both you and the person or group are able and willing to describe reality as it is.

As we have seen in chapter 2 on performance patterns, seeing and acknowledging reality is a bit more challenging than we might expect it to be because people tend to react to the emotional conflict they feel.

Your job is to let reality stand firmly in place. Imagine letting it "hang in the air," as it were, without trying to do anything with it *prematurely.* This makes it easier for a person or team to absorb the facts and then clearly acknowledge reality.

Like our direct reports, we will want to get the heat off, soften the blow, move on as quickly as we can. A better approach is to spend as much time as it takes for the person or team to acknowledge reality. One way to do that is to be very clear that we are putting in the foundation, which is reality, and we can achieve that first step by staying on topic.

Revisit an objective description of reality as needed.

During the flow of an MMOT, it might seem that the person is fully aware of the situation that you are describing, and yet later during the same talk, he may seem to lose touch with some of the facts. We saw an example of that in chapter 3 with Trish's team. Reality needed to be redescribed and reacknowledged several times. *Anytime* the person or team seems not to fully acknowledge reality, it is important to revisit it again. This sends the message, "We are going to look at reality exactly as it is and not pretend it is somehow different from how it is. We are using reality as a platform from which to build." Also we are delivering the message, "Reality is not going to be forgotten or swept under the table. We are here to address it and understand it."

Get a definitive yes or no. Is the description of reality accurate or not?

A very good basic technique is this: after you have stated reality, ask if the person agrees with you.

"The deadline for this report was last Tuesday, and it's now Friday. Is that correct?"

"The quality of this ad campaign is not up to our usual standard. Do you agree?"

"Your team didn't have the data they were assigned to bring to the meeting. Right?"

These questions require a simple yes or no. It is amazing how often people do not answer a yes-or-no question with "yes" or "no." If the person begins to give you a long explanation, you can remind her nicely that you are looking for a yes-or-no answer to the question you asked because at this point you are making sure you are on the same page about the facts. Often the explanations are about how reality got to be that way, rather than acknowledging how it actually is. Your tone and spirit of exploration are important here because you don't want to come across as a courtroom prosecutor conducting an adversarial cross-examination.

Watch out for qualified answers.

If the report was due on Tuesday and now it's Wednesday, the report is a day late. If the report is not fully complete by the due date, no matter how close it is to being done, it is not fully complete. If the subject of the MMOT tries to qualify the answer, you must make sure the facts stand without ambiguity.

"The report was not complete on the due date, Tuesday. Is that right?"

"Well, it was mostly done. I just had to put some finishing touches on it."

"But, still, it wasn't done on Tuesday, even though it was close to being done, right?"

"Right."

Watch out for a difference of opinion.

Sometimes there is a difference of opinion between you and the subject of the MMOT. Usually differences do not concern due dates, which are definitive. More often they might occur around quality issues. In thinking about quality, we need to know who is accountable for setting the standards. Is it the market? Is it senior management? Are you the one who sets the standards? It is hard to have an MMOT conversation around quality if it is unclear what the standards are and who sets them.

"This report is not up to our usual standards. Do you agree?"

"No. I think it is not only up to our usual standards, I think it's better."

This clear "no" reflects a difference of opinion, which will be followed by a useful discussion of the details concerning each opinion. What are the standards? Who sets them? What is the basis for each opinion? Are there objective standards to which we can refer?

When there is a difference of opinion, be open to understanding the other opinion. After hearing the person out, you may change your mind. If you change your mind and now agree that the quality is acceptable, the situation is resolved. If you don't agree, even though the person may not change her mind, you may decide that yours is the standard that must be met. The MMOT will likely lead to a clearer sense of the commission the person has been asked to accomplish and who is setting the standard for quality.

"Now that we've talked, we can see that you and I have very different standards around quality. I'm glad we've had a chance to have this discussion because it shows us where we might have future misunderstandings. Frankly, I must let you know that in these cases, it is my quality standards that we'll use. Part of my job responsibilities is to set these standards, and so that's what I'll be doing. I understand that if you were making the quality decisions, you would set the mark at a different point. However, let's both understand that I'll be setting them, and your job is to meet them. Are there any questions about that?"

Exploring a difference of opinion

In the following example, the manager explores the thought process of the direct report in order to understand her opinion. The manager is moving into step two for a moment, but this is not a "real" step two. Rather it is done to better understand reality and why this person has a different opinion about the quality.

"We are seeing this differently. In what ways does this report meet the standards?"

"It is clear, the graphics are great, and the production quality is first rate."

"Yes, all that's true, but the content doesn't communicate the conclusions we've reached, and there's a lot of material that just looks like filler, like the marketing research. Why did we put so much general research in that doesn't address our real customers or our real market?"

"For background."

"Why do we need to go into the background info in so much detail? And why the general market rather than our part of the market?"

"I guess we could have lived without it."

"When you decided to put it in, how did you think about it?"

"I wanted to make sure no one could say we didn't do a 'deep dive.'"

"I see. So it is in there to preempt criticism?"

"In a way."

"But that's not the point of the report. We are trying to give the readers relevant data on the issues we actually face. Right?"

"Right."

"By adding all this research, is the report clearer or less clear?"

"Well, now that you mention it, I suppose it is not as clear with all that research in there, especially since it wasn't part of the specs."

"Do you see why I think the reports are not up to our usual standards?"

"Yes, I do."

"Given what we just talked about, is that the case? In other words, is the report up to our usual standards, content and all?"

"No, given that we put in all of that superfluous market research, no."

"So we agree that the report is not up to our usual standards?"

"Yes."

Recognize the quick deflective "yes."

Not all "yeses" are created equal. Sometimes people quickly agree as a way of getting the heat off. You need to discern the difference between truly acknowledging reality and simply deflecting it. Here are a few useful tips:

- Notice if the person *consistently* shows she understands reality. If the person seems to vacillate, waver, or seem indecisive about the facts, then the quick agreement was probably used as deflection rather than as a real agreement.
- Notice if the person is interested in exploring his managerial process accurately, fairly, objectively, and openly. If he isn't, the first quick yes was probably deflective.
- Watch out for excuses and blaming others. If that is the case, the quick first yes was probably deflection.
- If you suspect that the first yes was deflective, ask the person

directly: *"You said yes very quickly, but now you seem to be imply-ing something else. How come?"* This type of straightforward question can help deepen the territory you both are exploring.

• Be open to changing your description of reality if new facts are introduced. Sometimes your understanding of reality may need to be updated:

"The report was due on Tuesday and now it's Wednesday."
"Well, actually, we changed the due date last week, and I sent you an e-mail letting you know that."

In this example, the facts change the situation being addressed. It is important to update your impression of reality as the facts re-quire.

With questions of fact—due dates, data, specifications—if there is a disagreement about what reality is, you both can review the infor-mation. But when it comes to qualitative opinions, there might be a legitimate difference of opinion. The person may think that the quality of work is fine when you do not. You need to be open to un-derstanding another point of view without giving up your own stan-dards

STEP TWO: TRACKING THE THOUGHT PROCESS
The blow-by-blow

Once we begin to analyze the process that led to the situation we have acknowledged, it is important to understand the sequence of events. A "blow-by-blow" can enable us to track the critical decisions that were made. When we identify the decision points, we can use them to track the logic the person was using. Were these the right decisions? Often, at the time, some decisions that turn out to be un-fortunate seem to be the best ones to make. Hindsight may be 20/20 because, at that point, we know if our assumptions were correct, we know the consequences of our actions, we know what the unforeseen events were that we could not predict, and we know the impact of our decisions. Hindsight is a great teacher. We can use it to discipline our general understanding of the conditions under which we make critical decisions. We can learn general principles such as trends, patterns, unexpected events that, nonetheless, can be expected. Most experienced engineering groups know that their development schedule will take longer than their plan. They can't predict exactly what factors will take longer than they thought, but they know the percentage of time it will happen. Their insight comes from all of the times they had unexpected delays. They write in additional time for a reasonable percentage of delays in their subsequent planning. This is the experience of hindsight that leads to a more productive performance pattern.

The easiest method to track the story is chronologically—from beginning to end.

"When you got the assignment, what was the first thing you did?"
"And then what did you do?"

Words into pictures

As you hear the story, one of the most effective techniques you can use is to translate the words you are hearing into pictures. Imagine you had a film crew in your head making a mental movie of the events the person is describing. This is a very effective way of putting yourself in the shoes of the person and experiencing what it was like when she made her decisions.

But don't stop there. Also picture what it was like being in the shoes of the other people in the story. This way, you can get a sense of the counterpoint that was in play.

Can you picture what happened? If you can, you create a higher level of understanding. If you can "see" some of the pictures but not others, you can then ask some very focused questions:

"You know, I can picture what happened until you talked about the contract dispute. And I really want to get a picture of what happened with that. Can you go over that part again so I can really get a sense of what happened?"

As you track the story, make your film, fill in the pictures as you get the information, ask questions when there are missing bits. Ask questions when things don't make sense logically.

Avoid speculating.

We all have the tendency to fill in the blanks when we don't have information we need. It is human nature to speculate. Speculation fills in the holes and connects the dots, imposing a sense of order and understanding. Unfortunately, too often our speculations and theories blind us to reality. When we think we know, we don't ask important questions.

Filling in the pictures with your own conjecture makes it hard to get the real story. It takes intellectual rigor to let the holes stand out in sharp relief. This is one of those counterintuitive skills that must be developed if we are to delve into the story of what really happened.

Fact: we know what we know; we don't know what we don't know. When we speculate or theorize, we are pretending to know what we don't know. Instead of filling the holes with synthetic padding, make a point of shining a spotlight in those areas. In our experience, the detective work reveals some of the most critical content you need for your analysis.

Assumptions

As you are tracking the story, you will discover some of the assumptions the person was making. What are these assumptions? Are they true?

Often people take action based on their assumptions rather than on reality as it is. When you are able to track the person's assumptions, you have access to a major force for change. If the assumptions are incorrect, as they often are, we can enable the person to look more carefully at reality next time. If the assumptions are generally true but not true in this instance, the person must also be more careful about studying reality and not rely on past experience or beliefs.

Assumptions are a product of thinking we know something to be true without looking to see if, in fact, it is. Sometimes our assumptions work well, and we do not need to reexamine them. But often the critical limitations to higher performance are found in the assumptions people make.

An example of such an assumption happened to the head of Sales for an international manufacturing company. He had been with the organization for over thirty years. During that time his industry had changed, the type of salespeople he had under him and the nature of sales management had changed. The only thing that didn't change were his assumptions about his role. The process he had used to create triumph after triumph was no longer successful. His people were afraid to tell him facts he needed to know. He became more frustrated and less effective. Yet once he had discovered the flaws in his assumptions about his job and his people, he was able to make a major shift. He had assumed that he needed to pressure his people to "make the numbers." In fact, the more pressure he put on them, the more they resisted his attempts to help them. His years of experience were valuable to them, but they were so busy avoiding his management style, he couldn't share his wisdom. He assumed they didn't want to know what he knew, so he had to force it down their throats. In fact, they did want to learn from him but were afraid to ask him for advice.

When he became aware of his assumption, he could test it out. In reality, his people did or did not want to learn from his experience. In reality, they did want to learn from him.

He held another assumption about his position. He thought of his job as an overseer of a group of unruly young salespeople. When he had a chance to rethink this assumption, we saw that they were young, but not unruly, just inexperienced. No amount of overseeing would enable them to get better. They really needed a mentor, and, as it turned out, he was the perfect person. Once we understood the assumption he was using as contrasted with reality, he changed his understanding of his job and become a mentor for his people. And he became a very effective manager and leader for the sales team and the organization.

What assumptions are built into the person's thought process? Are they true? How do we know?

Are we imposing generalizations on reality, or are we studying the specific reality we are in? Most people are not particularly rigorous in making this distinction. They fuse facts with concepts, past experiences, biases, and memories.

When dealing with assumptions, reality is the touchstone of truth. People make assumptions when they don't actually know the facts. The function of assumptions—the same as theories, speculations, and conjectures—is to create a sense of logic, even when we do not know what actually took place. Since so much of our thinking is influenced by the assumptions we make, we are on firmer ground when we test them against reality.

Reality is not always obvious. Sometimes we need to dig out facts, study relationships, go beneath the surface to the underlying dynamics. This is one of the essential disciplines in becoming more effective, creative, and flexible.

But too often we must make decisions without the benefit of knowing reality. When that is the case, it is helpful to know as much as we can and understand our past patterns. How often have our assumptions been correct in the past? When they haven't, what was the cause? What can we learn from these patterns?

Separate reality from assumptions so they do not seem to fuse. For some people, their assumptions are so ingrained, they cannot tell the difference between reality and what they invent based on their assumptions.

Design flaws

When you are tracking the person's story, become sensitive to how well the process or structural design worked. Often, people focus only on execution issues and ignore the importance of design. The discipline of system dynamics studies aspects of design complexity that often lead to limitations on growth and performance. MIT's Dr. Jay Forrester pioneered much of this work in the 1950s and 1960s. For our purposes, it is not necessary to explore systems issues, yet we do want to cite some of the wisdom that has been described by MIT's system dynamics group, some of it portrayed in Peter M. Senge's groundbreaking book *The Fifth Discipline*. Here are a few snapshots.

- Causes and symptoms are rarely close in time or space.
- Things aren't always what they appear to be.
- The solution to a problem often makes matters worse.
- When you try to push down on one part of a system, there is compensation in another part of the system.

These insights are not intuitive. We usually think that cause and effect are closely related in time. We usually think that events are caused by the immediately preceding events. We usually think that problem solving makes matters better. We usually think we can force our will to generate a change of pattern.

"Why did you decide to lower the quality of the product?"
"The competition was lowering prices. So we needed to lower our prices."

This simplistic answer is typical of *"event causes event"* thinking. Decisions to lower prices driven by market pressures can lead, as they might in the above example, to making the match between the offering and the market motivation both closer and further apart simultaneously. The price may be closer, but the quality may be further apart. In making such critical decisions, we need to see the broader design issues involved. In this example, responding to pricing pressures may lead to disgruntled customers. Since we made the change to make our customers happy, not angry with us, our "solution" has made matters worse. This can lead to another one of the insights listed above: when you push down on one part of a system, another part of the system compensates and seems to push back up.

Design issues concern the relationship of the parts to the whole. Often we see the telltale signs of design issues when a particular performance pattern consistently dogs a position, no matter who is in the role. A common experience within most organizations is this: a person is not performing well. We do everything we can think of to help the person. At last, we give up and replace that person with a new person. Within six months, the new person is behaving exactly like her predecessor.

Most people know of such situations, but we usually don't consider the implications of these types of situations. The most astonishing implication is that most things we hear from experts about human motivation turn out not to apply in these situations. After all, the new people in the same position acted similarly to their predecessors and yet they have many different personal characteristics.

Why do people do what they do? We may say it's their upbringing, or their education, or their environment. It's their cultural background or their IQ or their "emotional IQ." It's their DNA, or their astrology, or their numerology. Whatever we say are the factors that determine people's behavior, *none of them are as powerful or influential as the underlying structural dynamics that are built into the design of some positions within our organizations.*

When we see such consistent patterns of behavior emerge from vastly different people in the same position, we know we are dealing with design issues and not execution issues.

As we track the story of what happened in what sequence, be open to the elements of design as an important causal factor.

Unexpected events

Some events truly cannot be foreseen and planned. This is part of life. In these cases, we want to study how the person dealt with these events. How did he think about the situation? What decisions did he make? What did he learn? How did he plan to stay on course given the event? What did he do to rethink the situation?

The answers to these types of questions give us insight into how the person manages change and surprises. Some people are very good with routine, but do not do as well when the routine is broken. Others come alive when challenges stimulate their creative juices and produce brilliant performances. Hindsight may give us many invaluable lessons to ponder.

STEP THREE: CREATE A PLAN
<u>Rethinking the management process</u>
Once we understand the story of how it came to pass that the outcome was what it was, we are ready to put that insight into action by constructing a new management plan. Step three does four important things:

- It demonstrates the degree of learning the person has had by the way she rethinks her managerial approach.
- It creates a concrete plan for achieving a successful outcome next time.
- It creates a standard by which the person can be measured.
- It creates a context for further learning.

The proof of the pudding, goes the old adage, is in the eating. And so it is here. We can know if learning has occurred only when the person incorporates new actions and approaches into her managerial process. This new approach must be understood within the context of the lessons learned in step two. And it creates an understanding between the manager and the direct report. We know what the key elements are, and we are ready to emphasize them.

One of the best ways to enter into the planning process is to rethink how the person's approach would have changed if he knew then what is known now.

"If you had it to do all over again, same set of circumstances, given what we now know, how would you have approached this situation differently?"

We expect the person to give us insight that would have made the difference between a successful outcome and a less than successful outcome.

"I would have checked to see what the actual needs were, and I would have made sure that we didn't put excess marketing or any other superfluous information into the report."

"We would have made sure that everyone on the team was clear about the process we were using, and we would have managed our vendor relationship better."
"How would you have done that?"
"We would have assigned a particular individual to work with them closely. We would have driven their due dates more rigorously."
"How are you going to accomplish that? How's it going to be different this time?"
"I'm going to program my computer to send out alerts to my team to assure they're on track. And I'll follow up those alerts with e-mail or a phone call. And if it looks like it's going to be late, I can give people a heads-up."

This Monday morning quarterbacking can demonstrate the person's level of comprehension. Did he understand the factors that led to the outcome? Can he conceive of what needs to change? If the answer is yes, we are in good shape. But if the answer is no, we have more work to do, probably going back to step two. Further analysis can throw more light on the subject. Perhaps the story is clear to you but not to the person. Going back to step two will give you another chance to make sure you both understand the same events, their causes, and what's to be learned.

The next one
Another useful technique is to find out when the next similar project or event is going to occur. This will give us another chance to see if the person grasped the lessons available in step two.

"When is the next time you'll have a project like this?"
"Next month we have to analyze the prospect of opening a new product line in Asia."
"Given what we now know, how will you handle this one?"

We expect to see the learning from step two built into the new plans. If not, back to step two. If so, on to the new plan.

Picture the new plan

It is helpful to picture the new plan. Does it look like it can work? What are the built-in assumptions? Are they true? How do we know?

Your job at this point is to help the person think through the efficacy of the plan. What if this? What if that? You are not a "devil's advocate." Rather you are a scenario planner, helping the process of testing the practicality of the proposal. As you adjust the plan you strengthen your understanding of the plan. The person sees how you would think about it if it you were the author of the plan. The person can become aware of the general principles you bring to the thought process and how to translate those principles into actions. All of these actions are examples of mentorship.

Overall insights

Up to now, we are collecting insights. What are they? Often we can better understand the factors that need attention as well as the factors that are strengths that can be repeated or expanded. The plan is about the next time out. The insights are more general and able to be applied universally.

"Now that we've gone through this analysis and planning, what overall ideas or principles do you see that apply to you?"

STEP FOUR: THE FEEDBACK SYSTEM

The risk of the best plan is that it isn't implemented well. Plans are blueprints, not the finished product. There is truth in the view that the effectiveness of an organization is not the brilliance of its strategy but the brilliance of its executing against the strategy. Especially in industries where the nature of the product or service is easily replicated, speed, quality, and efficiency of execution become the strategic imperatives. This is one reason why Larry Bossidy and Ram

Charan make the argument in their book *Execution: The Discipline of Getting Things Done* that execution is strategic, not just tactical. Examples of organizations that are highly capable of magnificent execution include Dell, GE, UnitedHealth Group, and LaFrance, to name a few.

It is easy to leave the room having made arrangements with a sense of relief because we have mastered the performance challenge. We feel aligned in our resolve to change, and we believe we know how to do it. Wouldn't it be wonderful if it ended there and that's all it took? Unfortunately, that initial sense of relief and accomplishment we get is almost always temporary, although we may not know it at the time.

To prevent the MMOT from suffering the same fate, the fourth step—creating a feedback system—is critical. And the application of the feedback system is only as effective as it is consistent and rigorous. Monitoring the change in performance shouldn't be confused with micromanagement. On the contrary, it is the basic stuff of management. Managers don't make things, they make performance. So as a manager, my helping others improve performance *is* my primary responsibility. And having a real system of follow-up in place is essential to assure new behaviors are learned and that they stick. Ask yourself the question, "If the desired performance pattern didn't show up in the manager's behavior, how would I address it?" Most likely by putting out a system of steps that this time you would more closely monitor. The logic of this step is, why wait? The coach wouldn't wait to lose the next game before demanding additional team practice, and we shouldn't wait either if we expect new behaviors to become a part of an improved management discipline.

Having said rigorous application of this step is necessary, it needn't be a big deal. Periodic check-ins at key points, regular updates as part of normal staff meetings, quick phone calls or e-mails do the trick. At first it may feel like this is overdoing it—it isn't. Creating new managerial habits always takes more time in the beginning. However, when you see consistent constant improvement, adjust the oversight accordingly. As people improve, trust their performance and give them great opportunities. Even then, some over-sight and checking in will always be a part of the relationship.

The follow-up e-mail

An easy way to establish a system of follow-up is through e-mail. It gives you both a record of what was understood during the MMOT technique, what they learned, what insights they had. It is valuable, too, if you need a reference in a future MMOT.

Ask the person to write you an e-mail describing the main points. Their depth of learning will be apparent. When people put something in writing, they are often able to get a more tangible sense of what they learned. When you write what you know, you end up knowing more than you did. This is very much the case for the MMOT.

Agree on a deadline for the e-mail and in general make the date sooner (within three days) rather than later.

The conversation would be something like:

"Can you send me an e-mail describing our conversation? Include in it what happened and why, what we learned from that, what you'll do differently next time, and anything else that seems important to mention. That way, we'll both have a record of this talk."

"Sure."

"And can you have that to me by Tuesday of next week?"

"Yes, I can."

The follow-up

The new plan will consist of design elements, actions to take, decisions to make, others to manage, information to collect and distribute, and a host of other activities. Generally the implementation of the plan will have a beginning, a middle, and an end. For each plan, there will be critical events to watch carefully. It's important to check in with each other during these critical stages.

Short meetings are the best. But you must give them the time you need to be assured that the person is adopting a new performance pattern. A "How's it going?—Fine" exchange is not enough to get a sense of what's going on. You created a picture of the plan in step three, and now you can compare that picture with the reality of the plan.

"Where are we now in the process?"

"We just signed the contract with B. D. Carter and Sons."

"Was that on time?"

"No, it was a little late."

"What happened?"

"Their agent had to be out for a week when his wife had a baby, and that put things back a week."

"Are we behind a week for everything?"

"No. But a few things are off."

"How do you plan to deal with that?"

"I've asked my people to give me a new schedule and rearrange things a bit so we can make the date."

"Have you got it yet?"

"No. I gave them until next Thursday."

"Are your folks good at being flexible? I mean, do you think they'll sort it out?"

"They're usually not so good when we have to change things. I'm going to have to drive this a little more closely."

"What are your plans if they don't give you a new schedule that's workable?"

"To take what they've done and rework it myself."

"Tell you what. Why don't you bring it over once you've had a chance to rework it, and we can go over it? Sounds like something we should take a look at together."

"Good. That'll be helpful."

The above example shows how feedback often works. There may be regular check-ins. But often, the actual system dictates its own logic in relationship to feedback. We don't want to take the management burden on our own shoulders. If we do that, we will become overwhelmed and our capacity will run out awfully fast. We just want to help the person accountable succeed. We need to create a feedback system that, like Goldilocks's porridge, is not too much, not too little, but just right. You can only know what's "just right" when you work with your team within the context of specific projects or deliverables.

Feedback as mentoring

The best context for mentoring your team is within these feedback sessions. Sometimes, you may need to conduct another MMOT as part of the feedback. People hardly ever learn all they need to know in one conversation. Through a series of MMOTs, greater mastery comes. In the arts and in sports most people, even those at the top of their professions, have mentors, teachers, and coaches. We learn better when we can review what we've done, what we are currently doing, how we are thinking about it, and what we might consider that we haven't thought of on our own. Most people think they need to be "do-it-yourselfers." But that's usually the slowest and most difficult path to increasing your skills, insights, and performance. Once we get the idea that a little help is good, a new world of possibilities opens to us. We no longer have to go it alone. It's okay to get support. It's okay to talk shop. It's okay to see our professional life as a work in process and that we grow stronger from ongoing learning.

Another benefit from having a mentorship relationship is this: when you are in the thick of it, it is hard to back up and see the situation objectively. An important discipline is to view the situation from various vantage points. See it from a close-up angle and then back up and look at it from a greater distance or time frame. Look at it upside down, backward, and backward and upside down. By changing vantage points, we get a clearer fix on reality, generate more creative possibilities, and free ourselves from our own blind spots.

The MMOT Form

The MMOT form is flexible, but its logic is based on sequence. Before we can track new actions, we need to have a new plan. Before

we can create a better plan, we need to understand our previous performance. Before we can understand what happened, we need to recognize the actual reality we produced. The MMOT process creates
its own natural rhythm as you move from step to step. As you become more experienced in this process, you will learn how to master
the form in such a way that it will naturally flow. You will internalize
it. And the lessons will be absorbed into your overall management
style, in which factors of truth telling, exploring, seeing relationships
among parts, working collaboratively, and the spirit of support come
into play even when you are not formally conducting an MMOT.

5

The Positive Moment of Truth

As we have seen, the moment of truth consists of two events: an awareness of a difference between the actual and expected outcome, and the decisions you make to address or ignore the situation. Usually the difference concerns an outcome that does not meet our expectations. But sometimes the managerial moment of truth is the exact opposite—our expectations have been exceeded. We call these events the *positive moment of truth*.

The positive MMOT can be as powerful a learning experience as the corrective MMOT. Each of the steps may be used, although here the learning typically focuses on what worked particularly well and how we may adopt that approach in the future.

It is important for us to understand that the positive MMOT is not designed to be used simply as positive reinforcement. Sometimes the positive MMOT does have that added benefit. *But that's not the point of it*; that is simply a side effect. The point is to acknowledge and learn from something that's occurred.

The Motivation

It's one thing to give a compliment when it's true. But some managers liberally pass out compliments, even when they are not justified. We don't read their praise as credible. Since we perceive their flattery as patronizing, it's not even positive reinforcement.

When we conduct an MMOT to make corrections, we aren't addressing the issues at hand so the person will feel badly about himself. In a positive MMOT, we aren't addressing reality so the person will feel good.

From the broader organizational viewpoint, we want to create a platform for truth company-wide. To do that, we need to be clear about our motivation. We need to separate the act of seeing and telling the truth, on the one hand, from saying things for effect, on the other.

Telling the truth does not mean we have to adopt bad manners. We want to find accessible ways to express ourselves so that our words reflect our thoughts. But we need to be clear about *why* we are saying what we are saying. If we are not being honest with people, they know it.

When we start being straight with people, they may feel perplexed at first. If they are not used to others being candid with them, they may wonder what we are up to. But over time, they will see that we say what we mean and they can count on us to tell them the truth. From that point on, our words have more power and impact.

The moral of the story is this: be on the level. Then when we do compliment performance, it means something. People know it was said sincerely.

The motivation for the corrective and positive MMOT is exactly the same: to acknowledge reality and learn from it.

The Power of Public Acknowledgment of Good Work

While the positive moment of truth is not motivated by an attempt to create positive reinforcement, it is still an event that has actual positive reinforcing value.

The Form

With the positive MMOT, the four steps of the MMOT process are variations of the same theme: acknowledge reality, analyze how it got to be that way, plan for next time, create a feedback system.

Perhaps some of these steps are not as useful as they are during a corrective MMOT, but it is amazing how much practical learning we can generate by going through the form.

STEP ONE: ACKNOWLEDGE REALITY
First is the statement of fact.

"We expected you to open the Brazilian market with 5 percent market share, but you managed to achieve a 12 percent market share. Is that right?
"Yes."
"Well, well done. More than doubling your goal is a superb achievement."

Often reality includes that we are pleased the person or team has exceeded their goals. We want to acknowledge two things: the reality itself and our delight that the person or team has done so well.

Usually people find it easier to acknowledge a positive moment of truth than a corrective one. But many people deflect praise.

"This month sales are up by 22 percent above plan."
"Yeah, I guess we got lucky."

"We've noticed that your team released the product early and under budget."
"They're a good group."

These types of "aw-shucks" responses often are seen as good manners. Many people are taught not to brag about their accomplishments. However, the realm of truth demands that truth be told. Sometimes the truth is that the person did one hell of a job, and the outcome wouldn't have been as good had he not performed as well as he did.

Step one is about acknowledgment. As in a corrective MMOT, we need to do more than just announce reality. We need to get agreement about the difference between the expected result and the actual outcome. There isn't any difference in the form of step one, be it corrective or positive, except that the content is much more pleasant. Because of our dedication to creating a platform for truth in the organization, we are using the positive MMOT to deepen our understanding of reality. We are not simply complimenting work that was well done; we are mentoring, exploring the processes that led to the success, and learning what we can use in the future. In step two we will analyze how the person produced such great performance. Step one is simply acknowledgment of the performance.

> *"This month sales are up by 22 percent above plan."*
>
> *"Yeah, I guess we got lucky."*
>
> *"We'll take a look at how Lady Luck came into your life in a moment, but, just to make sure we agree, am I right about sales being up 22 percent above plan?"*
>
> *"Yes."*

STEP TWO: ANALYZE HOW IT HAPPENED

During this step in the positive MMOT, we track just how the person (or team) achieved the result. This is the same process as in the corrective MMOT. It may be useful to track the story by sequence: what happened first, and then what happened.

The sequencing technique is very useful when people have blind spots and can't see where they typically make their mistakes. Usually a blind spot does not contribute to an outstanding outcome as it does in a corrective MMOT. The person may have made good or well-executed decisions that were creative, flexible, and strategic. Perhaps we need to help the person move from "unconscious competence" to "conscious competence." There may be useful lessons that will be replicable.

One of the most common ways to address step two is to "cut to the chase"—in other words, ask the person how we can account for the performance.

> *"You know, this sales figure was much higher than we anticipated. Help me understand how it happened. What can we learn? What were some of the critical factors that led to this outcome?"*

This is both a focused and an open-ended question. We need to move from the "aw-shucks" explanations about "luck" or "we have a great team" to more tangible content.

"You said it was luck. What part of the result was produced because of luck, and what part has to do with performance?"

"You said it was because you had a good team. What did they do that really worked particularly well?"

Perhaps an outstanding result was a product of luck. Usually there are various circumstances that can fall in our favor. When that happens, it is hard to take the credit. But if it becomes a chronic pattern, we might ask, "How does it turn out that you folks are so lucky?" We may discover that some people make their own luck and we can learn from them.

STEP THREE: CREATE A PLAN

In the positive MMOT, the plan is usually about how we can institutionalize the insights we observed in step two. Too often, success doesn't succeed within organizations. New, highly workable processes are not duplicated in other parts of the organization. People may not apply the factors that made all of the difference last time to a similar situation next time.

When we talk about a learning organization, one thing we mean is that insights based on experiences can be deployed throughout the organization. This type of collective learning does not happen by itself. It is an organizational discipline and needs to be structured into the organizational learning process. In step three we are asking the person or team how they might use the insights they noticed in other work they do. Their answers shed light on how well they understand the critical factors of success. We may need to work with these insights so that we understand just what those factors were, how well we can generalize working principles from them, and how we can use these principles in other circumstances.

STEP FOUR: FEEDBACK

In the corrective MMOT, implementing a feedback system is essential if we are to manage a change of pattern. In the positive MMOT there is another reason for feedback: to test our impressions about what truly works and how we are using those factors in our work. We want the positive MMOT to lead to amplification or expansion of the factors. We want more and more people learning from them, adopting them, making them their own. We want the organization to have the ability to absorb the advancements of any member so that the individual learning experience becomes a collective learning experience for everyone.

Feedback may involve just how well we are using our newly acquired insights and practices. But it also may include spreading the word through organizational newsletters and e-mails to those who could benefit from the insights, and so on.

The positive MMOT is both another aspect of truth telling *and* a learning process that comes from an accurate view of reality. To some managers, truth telling is used only when the news is bad. The impact of that practice is to diminish honesty through the organization because a spin toward either a positive or negative view of reality ends up being a bias that distorts the facts. When we call it like it is, truth is articulated without bias or politics. This is the most powerful platform from which to advance the mission of the organization.

6

Case Study: Working Within the Cross-Functional Team

Since much of the important work in an organization is performed by cross-functional teams, it is critical we understand how the MMOT can make them highly effective. A cross-functional team, by definition, is made up of people from a variety of functional disciplines and business divisions to drive a project initiative or plan. They are typically temporary teams, coming in and out of existence based on the life of the project. They bring multiple skills to bear on work that cuts across the company and often needs to be understood from a broad-process point of view. Team members, often at different levels in the company, are chosen by their area of expertise.

One of the most complex professional relationships managers have is within the cross-functional team. They are asked to support common goals, but they must find the time and resources to do their respective parts. Too often the work of the cross-functional team is in conflict with the various projects their departments have. Bosses do not always agree with the plans that the cross-functional manager agrees to. The manager is not rewarded or measured by how well she succeeds on the cross-functional team. Too often, the manager who is assigned the work is put in a thankless position in which no matter how he plays it, he will lose something in the process. Yet cross-functional teams are needed to better coordinate projects that require input from various sources. How can the team work better than usual? We need to put the real issues on the table, which we can do using an MMOT. What would motivate anyone to respond cooperatively? The basic outcome the team has committed to is an organizing principle. Understanding the various forces in play that take us away from other competing objectives is another important issue that must be faced and dealt with.

In the following example, Sandy needs to coordinate with Bill, who seems never to be available to support the team deliverables, which are inextricably tied to the company's major market strategy.

Sandy calls Bill. After the preliminaries, the MMOT begins.

SANDY

"Okay, I need to see if we had the same impressions going out of the last cross-functional meeting."

BILL

"Okay."

SANDY

"Did we say we were going to meet the March 1 deadline for the VP.112?"

BILL

"Yup."

SANDY

"And did you say that you were going to get me the revised specs by last Friday?"

BILL

"Well, there's a lot going on."

SANDY

"For me, too. But I just want to make sure I got it right. You did say Friday, right?"

BILL

"Right."

SANDY

"Okay, Bill. Is this a good time to talk about this?"

BILL

"I've got a 3:30, so I've got maybe fifteen minutes."

SANDY

"Thanks. When did you know you weren't going to get me the specs on Friday?"

BILL

"When did I know? You mean, when did I say to myself, 'Gee, I'm going to miss that date?'"

SANDY

"Yup."

BILL

"Around Wednesday sometime, I think."

SANDY

"How did you think about letting me know?"

BILL

"I meant to have Jill on my staff call you. But I just got too swamped."

SANDY

"Why were the specs late?"

BILL

"Some of the data wasn't in. Charlie was sick last week, so we couldn't get his part done."

SANDY

"I see. Given that, how did you plan on getting me the specs?"

BILL

"It just slipped off the radar screen."

SANDY

"I imagine this kind of thing happens all the time."

BILL

"You imagine right."

SANDY

"Now, while we're on this project, I'm going to need a number of things from you. So let's figure this one out so we can work this out better in the future. Okay?"

BILL

"Okay."

SANDY

"You know, Bill, this is one of those managerial moments of truth we've all been working with. Right?"

BILL

"Right."

SANDY

"Do we agree that both of us are accountable for the March 1 due date of the VP.112?"

BILL

"Sure."

SANDY

"My part is off by a few days because I didn't get the specs."

BILL

"Well, you should receive them today. And I'm really sorry I didn't let you know last week. I should have given you a heads-up."

SANDY

"I appreciate that."

BILL

"So I got busy, Charlie was out, and I didn't let you know. Could I have done it differently? Besides letting you know, I don't know what else I could have done."

SANDY

"Well, to make the date, I need the specs."

BILL

"I know."

SANDY

"And this type of thing is going to happen throughout this project, I imagine."

BILL

"It's bound to."

SANDY

"Should we try to change the March 1 due date?"

BILL

"We can't."

SANDY

"Are we going to be late?"

BILL

"I guess we'll do what we always do, pull all-nighters near the end."

SANDY

"That gets a little old."

BILL

"Yup."

SANDY

"Is this a design thing? I mean, have we got the right process?"

BILL

"Maybe not."

SANDY

"If we can pull it off with all-nighters at the end, you've got to figure that we could spread some of those hours over the weeks we have left."

BILL

"Yeah."

SANDY

"What kinds of things do we need to do?"

BILL

"Now that you mention it, we could move up the packaging design work, and then we'd get that out of the way. That's one that always is left hanging."

SANDY

"Okay. That's good."

BILL

"Then hire a few temps to add some support to programming."

SANDY

"Do we have budget for that?"

BILL

"We do. We don't usually use it, but we do and we can."

SANDY

"How about we work out a better logistical plan before the next cross-functional meeting?"

BILL

"You and me? Or do we need a few other people there?"

SANDY

"Well, Ron needs to be in on this."

BILL

"Right. You want to set it up?"

SANDY

"Sure. Now, I'm going to send you an e-mail about this talk so we both have a record of it."

BILL

"Good."

SANDY

"And I'll set up a meeting for a few of us to redesign the process we're using."

BILL

"Good."

SANDY

"But, also, let's keep in touch during this process. I know we're all busy, but we better not lose touch with each other."

BILL

"You're right. How about setting up a weekly check-in, you know, five minutes every Tuesday, that kind of thing?"

SANDY

"Sounds great. So here's what we've said. We're all busy, and we can see what's going to happen if we don't change things, like all-nighters, and that's a bummer. A few of us are going to redesign the process so we have a better chance to pull this off without killing ourselves. We'll get to packaging right away, since that's something that can take us off track if we begin that too late, and we'll touch base for a few minutes every week just to make sure we're on track."

BILL

"Yeah. Great. Sounds good."

SANDY

"Thanks for this talk."

BILL

"You too. I'd better get going."

SANDY

"Me too. Bye."

BILL

"See you."

Using the MMOT with cross-functional teams can make the difference between success and failure. Well-designed cross-functional teams have an owner with clear authority. That authority isn't determined by hierarchical reporting relationships but by defining the best place to assign a performance outcome. Using the MMOT with a cross-functional team is driven ultimately by the requirement of the project and the commitment to the team, not one's title. If used well, the MMOT in a cross-functional setting creates a level of performance expectation that is driven by my responsibility to turn out great work. In using the four steps of the MMOT in a cross-functional team, the team leader's pursuit of the four steps will rely on getting acknowledgment on how my behavior is affecting our performance. It is here that peer group influence can be a powerful motivation in changing behavior. Each team member will expect the others to carry their own weight. Often the MMOT will be with a team leader and team member. Equally effective can be a candid team MMOT that looks at all the interlinking responsibilities of the team. Like other team MMOTs, these discussions aren't easy. If done with current reality as its foundation and common acknowledgment and commitment to the team's ultimate outcome, great things can happen. Blaming others turns into taking responsibility, and initiatives are achieved on time and on budget.

7

The Art of the Question: Exploring Reality

There are four types of questions that we can use during the MMOT to better penetrate reality: *information, clarification, implication,* and *discrepancy.*

The Information Question

The *information* question is designed to expand the picture we are forming when we conduct an MMOT. Often it is used to add detail or expand the frame through which we are looking. As the name suggests, this type of question is looking for additional information for better understanding.

"The team set the due date."
"What's the date?" (Information question)

"Last week the numbers went up."
"What were the numbers?" (Information question)

"We just hired a replacement for Sue."
"Whom did you hire? When does she start?" (Information questions)

Information questions are designed to fill in the picture with accurate information. In the following example, the information questions help the person tell the story:

"So I told John he has to deliver on time from now on."

"What did he say?" (Information question)

"He said he would try."

"What did you tell him after he said that?" (Information question)

"I told him that frankly trying isn't good enough. We are counting on that delivery date, and if it is late, it'll throw us off schedule."

"What did he say then?" (Information question)

"He said that everyone has problems, but he'd do his best."

"How did you respond to that?" (Information question)

"I told him if he couldn't deliver on time, we'd find someone who could."

"Can we find another vendor?" (Information question)

"Yeah, we think so."

"Have you checked around?" (Information question)

"Larry did. He said there were a few good choices."

"How did you leave it with John?" (Information question)

"He said he would try. He didn't commit."

"What will you do?" (Information question)

"Try out some of the other vendors for the next few orders and see if we can get someone more reliable."

Notice how each question helped expand the picture.

Because we are exploring reality factually, most of the questions we will ask in an MMOT exercise will be information questions. We are forming a picture of what happened and why it happened. We are tracking relationships among the various factors in the story. We are interested in finding out the essential decision points that the person made. We are interested in the responses to those decisions. We want to know what actions were taken and what the results of those actions were.

The Clarification Question

Often, people use terms that are unclear to the listener and, perhaps, even to the speaker herself. Usually, we don't ask the person to define these terms. Instead, we pretend we know exactly what she means. This is a habit we developed in school. Because we were rewarded for knowing and penalized for not knowing, when we didn't know, we pretended to know. We learned that it was better to fake it.

We were not encouraged to ask questions about how a term was being used or what it meant in a particular context. If we did, it made us look like we didn't study, or use a dictionary, or understand the most basic context that everyone else seemed to comprehend.

When people enter the organizational world, the same norm is in place. People commonly use terms that are imprecise, undefined, and, occasionally, meaningless. Yet most everyone colludes with each other by pretending to understand what is being said.

Business jargon is an enormous bastion of fuzziness. How often have we heard terms such as *quality, customer focused, core competencies, deep dive, process management, excellence,* and *knowledge management* used vaguely and impressionistically without any clear meaning in sight. Terms like these are used as a shorthand code, but the codebook got lost years ago. These types of terms once may have had real meanings but now have become banal.

Take a seemingly innocuous term such as *quality.* Exactly what does it mean?

The notion of *quality* has come very far from Dr. W. Edwards Deming's brilliant system of building superior quality into the manufacturing lines by minimizing variances through improved processes. As a statistician, Deming created an *exacting* approach to measuring the effectiveness that processes had on predictable levels of quality. From such understanding, people could redesign their manufacturing processes, and the outcome was dramatic: lower cost, higher quality, more control, less variation, and fewer defects. Deming wanted people to become more thoughtful, inventive, and observant. He saw mindlessness as an enemy to high performance and mindfulness as the key to achieving higher performance. Organizational performance is mediocre at best when managers follow by rote and do not understand the reasons for the actions they take or the underlying purpose, content, or context of those actions.

Fast-forward twenty years and the quality movement is nothing more than a memory. Twenty years before, many organizations had VPs in charge of quality. Not many of those positions survived the 1990s. What remains of the quality movement is plagued with many artifacts that, ironically, are the opposite of what Deming advocated. Thoughtfulness is replaced by the practice of filling out bureaucratic forms. *Quality* became less about building a high level of quality within a product and more about winning awards, such as the Malcolm Baldridge National Quality Award in America. Original and creative thinking, through which the organization was to build quality into its approach, was transposed into a mechanical, bureaucratic process, one without a real focus on the outcome: higher-quality products and services. When people use the word *quality* nowadays, what do they mean? Sometimes they have very specific ideas they are attempting to express, but too often they do not know what they are trying to say.

The pattern of something useful being neutralized into something hollow is not uncommon. We are well aware that something as powerful as the Managerial Moment of Truth can become a catchphrase that misses the point. It takes true discipline to support substance over manner. And the clarification question helps people by asking them to make clear what might otherwise be fuzzy.

The need to define our terms has never been more relevant than in our contemporary organizational life. For example, someone called "Morgan" offered the following statement as part of a contest on the Internet. Here was his challenge:

Win $100
The first person to e-mail a one-paragraph summary (150 words or fewer) clearly explaining what, exactly, this company—JargiCorp [name changed to protect the innocent]—does will receive a check of **$100** from me.

E-mail all entries and questions [to Morgan—no longer available].
Good luck!

JargiCorp: Dedicated to Excellence

One of JargiCorp's corporate objectives is to develop strategic relationships with key customers and be recognized for our ability to deliver services of superior value. This competitive advantage will be
achieved through continued focus on our core competencies, management attention to the development of operations and process
management excellence in all parts of our business, the identification
and application of best processes, and continued attention to direct
and indirect cost management. The focus on core competencies will
promote the concentration of knowledge in select areas consistent
with the tenets of JargiCorp's strategic plan, JargiCorp 2000. Management's attention to operations and process management excell-
lence in all business areas will be achieved through the continued
expansion of our management and technical staff, as well as through
consistent application of corporate quality programs such as bench-
marking and continuous improvement, leading to the establishment
of JargiCorp's superior business processes in each core competency.
Finally, continued attention to direct and indirect cost management
will enable JargiCorp to offer customers a superior, value-added
package of high-quality service at a competitive price.

As we look to the twenty-first century, JargiCorp's goals will be to
penetrate new markets, attract external equity financing, and achieve
increased business volume. Our most critical challenges will involve
moving faster, communicating better, and coordinating activities
more closely companywide. We must concentrate on growth within
our existing clients and seek to improve upon the ways in which we
solicit new business. We must question old ways of marketing while
consistently fine-tuning our selling processes. Our future success will
depend largely upon the quality of our service and our ability to
leverage additional work from existing contacts.

Our strengths to date have been built on a strong commitment to
quality, value, integrity, and innovation. Management must continue

to invest in the appropriate technology, human resources, and infra-structure to meet our strategic goals and objectives. We must con-tinue to deliver high-quality, value-added services by hiring only the best and the brightest professionals. We must retain, motivate, and reward these individuals and instill in them an unmatched commit-ment to client service.

JargiCorp will face many challenges in 2000. Successfully manag-ing these challenges will demand a strong commitment from Jargi-Corp's senior management. We must invest in new technology to strengthen our performance management and control processes. In order to effectively manage the day-to-day operations of JargiCorp, management must have immediate access to relevant financial and operational information. We must capitalize on our own experiences and expertise. Understanding how to leverage our internal knowl-edge is no longer simply an advantage—it's a business imperative. JargiCorp's ability to learn faster than its competitors is quickly be-coming its strongest sustainable competitive edge.

A critical initiative beginning in 2000 will involve organizing our internal knowledge, best practices, and innovations into an effective knowledge management system. Building upon our proven method-ology for continuous quality improvement, JargiCorp will combine resources to develop a corporate learning system. The system will as-sist our professionals in staying abreast of current company goals, ob-jectives, and strategies and will enable JargiCorp as a whole to provide a higher level of customer service through the sharing of val-idated knowledge management processes.

JargiCorp has recognized the need to develop a new strategy de-signed to diversify its customer base by expanding into newer, faster-growing, and more profitable markets.

Corporate Vision

JargiCorp is committed to providing value-added services through the growth of personal and business relationships that translate into com-petitive profits, client satisfaction, professional growth and career en-hancement for our employees, and long-term viability for the company.

Corporate Mission

Our multifaceted mission is our driving force. JargiCorp wants to:

1. Establish solid corporate leadership which guides and directs the effective accomplishment of strategic goals and objectives;
2. Foster an attitude of outstanding customer service and satisfaction;
3. Continually refine our corporate vision to leverage our human, technical, and financial resources effectively to achieve strategic goals;
4. Instill a corporate atmosphere, management philosophy, and organizational performance criteria which capitalize on diversity;
5. Promote a commitment to outstanding performance, quality, innovation, and pursuit of excellence; and
6. Maintain a people-come-first environment where all employees are integral components of our success formula.

When we consider extreme cases, we can get a sense of the more subtle manifestation of the same dynamic in operation, even when it is less obvious. Unintelligible as the above statement is, it is not far from what we hear in most of the world's largest corporations. Companies that become hypnotized by such verbiage can't truly understand what is being said. And yet the game is to pretend to understand it all. No one wants to be the first to admit that he doesn't understand what everyone else seems to grasp so easily. No one with a mind to further his career wants to be the kid who points out that the emperor has no clothes, especially if the emperor is the one handing out the promotions, bonuses, career advancement, more responsible positions, and more interesting work assignments.

Here are a few examples of a clarification question helping to define imprecise or unknown terms:

"We need a more customer-focused approach."
"Just what do we mean by customer focused in this case?"

"We just got a PJK report.*"*
"What is a PJK report*?"*

"The competition is ahead in the core competencies *war."*
"How are you defining core competencies *in this regard?"*

"We need more leadership *in the ranks."*
"I know what those terms mean, but I'm not quite sure of what you have in mind. Could you say what you have in mind?"

Clarification questions encourage people to be more precise. The answers help us know what we are talking about. The practice sends everyone the message that it's okay to ask questions when we don't know. It's not okay to pretend we know when we don't.

The Implication Question

Often people imply information, ideas, notions, assumptions, concepts, and their own opinions rather than simply telling us explicitly what they think. Too often we have learned to hide our actual thoughts. This is another factor that makes it hard to get at the truth. While a very strong cultural habit in most organizations, it is one of which most people are unaware.

In other words, most people are innocent of guile. They are just not terribly aware of the assumptions they make or the concepts they hold. They communicate their underlying assumptions by implication.

In day-in-day-out management, we find assumptions expressed as implications. Because implications are less obvious than direct statements, we often ignore them. But through the implication question, we can learn how to address underlying assumptions so that they become addressable.

"Do you actually think Bob is the right guy to lead this project?" (Implication: Bob isn't.)
Implication question: "What reservations do you have?"

"You can't always ask people to be perfect." (Implication: We are demanding too much.)
Implication question: "Do you think we are being too demanding?"

"He finally got it right. (Implication: in the past he didn't get it right.)
Implication question: "Is that unusual?"

Implication questions help put a topic more fully on the table so we can address the whole story. If we record most meetings and then analyze what is being said, we will find that much of the discussion occurs in subtext—in other words, in implication. By asking implication questions, subtext becomes text, and we can more easily explore the topic area.

The implication question has two distinct steps: recognize what is being implied, and ask the person if it is true.

It is a curious fact that many people do not always agree with what they are implying. The assumption or opinion is so built into the fabric of their thinking, they don't even know it's there. When the implication is pointed out, they may agree or disagree with it. The implication question gives them a chance to rethink some of their basic assumptions and concepts.

Here is an example of a typical implication question:

"We got into the marketplace too late."

STEP ONE: WHAT IS IMPLIED?

In the above statement, what is implied is that had they gotten into the marketplace earlier, they would have had more success. Knowing this idea is built into the statement, we can move to step two: asking the implication question.

STEP TWO

"Had we gotten into the marketplace earlier, would we have been more successful?"

If the person agrees with the implication, we expect the answer to be yes. But the person may not actually agree with the implication that success would have been forthcoming had they entered the market sooner. In either case, the implication question opens the door to getting at fundamental assumptions, concepts, and beliefs. Some of the most extraordinary insights and creativity come from these types of explorations.

Often we don't know what we assume. We think our assumptions are so true that they go without question. And so, they are not questioned, but rather fixed into our thought process. We can be blind to these notions. We think of them as givens. We may not see them, but we let ourselves stand on them for support and a sense of orientation. Moments of truth sometimes lead to a spotlight illuminating our assumptions. Sometimes our assumptions stand up to such rigorous scrutiny. But often we come to realize we are standing on quicksand. In light of day, our assumptions do not hold up. These moments can feel rather disorienting, because the underpinning of our sense of security is suddenly and unceremoniously overthrown.

One of the most exciting moments in life is to rethink an old assumption and change one's mind. Scientific advancement, for an example, repeatedly has been generated from rethinking old assumptions and coming to new conclusions. The great creative scientists generated new insights, often over the dogmatic convictions of true believers in unexamined ideas from the past. We need only think of Galileo, Newton, and Einstein to see how the history of science was dramatically changed when old assumptions were challenged and rethought. Thomas Kuhn, in *The Structure of Scientific Revolutions*, put it this way: "And when it does—when, that is, the profession can no longer evade anomalies that subvert the existing tradition of scientific practice—then begin the extraordinary investigations that lead the profession at last to a new set of commitments, *and new basis for the practice of science*. The extraordinary episodes in which that shift of professional commitments occurs are the ones known in this essay as scientific revolutions. They are the tradition-shattering complements to the tradition-bound activity of normal science." If this principle is such an advantage to science, think of how much value rethinking old assumptions can have within the organization, an institution in which people are encouraged to adopt the party line intellectually.

Most business innovations come from rethinking old assumptions. Most new effective business strategies come from rethinking the nature of the industry. Most revolutionary business advancements are the product of exploring the old assumptions, putting them under the microscope, testing their validity, and from this rigor, generating a new approach that those who clung to the past couldn't have imagined. Think of how markets have changed, sometimes knocking out the industry giants. It is almost hard to remember that at one point Wang owned the word-processing market and Digital Equipment and IBM owned the computer industry. The personal computer changed marketplace dynamics and changed the world by imagining everyone owning a computer. Amazon.com rethought book distribution, and now many in the entertainment business are rethinking how to deliver their products online. Steve Jobs, a stellar example of a visionary business leader rethinking old assumptions, destroyed the Sony Walkman's domination with the iPod.

The Discrepancy Question

Sometimes people contradict themselves. The discrepancy question is designed to sort out these contradictions. Here is an example:

"Last year we had a great year. Sales were down."

There is an apparent contradiction between great year and lower sales. How are we to understand this discrepancy? There are only two possibilities: either one or both statements are untrue, or there is missing information that explains the apparent discrepancy.

One statement is incorrect:

"How can we have had a great year if sales were down?" (Discrepancy question)

"Did I say we had a great year? No, that was the year before. Last year was a disaster."

Or:

"Did I say sales were down? Sales were up."

Or there is information that explains the apparent discrepancy.

"We had a great year because we obtained our patent, and all of our competitors have to pay us royalties. So our actual sales don't matter because we make money from everyone selling that type of product."

Here's another example:

"Bill's the right guy to lead the project, although he has poor people skills and doesn't communicate well."
"Since Bill has poor people skills and doesn't communicate well, why is he the right guy to lead the project?" (Discrepancy question)

One part of the discrepancy is not true:

"Did I say Bill has poor people skills? No, that was John. Bill has very good people skills and communicates well."
"Did I say Bill was the right guy for the job? He is the worst person we could get."

Or there's information that explains the apparent discrepancy:

"Bill is the only one who knows the system we are reengineering. Plus, he can do it with minor support from the team."

In the above examples the discrepancy is in the same paragraph. Usually discrepancies occur over a much longer time frame. The person may say one part of the discrepancy half an hour before stating the contradiction. If we are listening closely, the discrepancy will stand out, even if it is separated by time.

Working with the group

The discrepancy question can also be used when you are working with a management team. Members do not always agree. Advocates of different positions stake out their territory. They then argue about whose position is the correct one. During these sessions people do not listen well to those with a different point of view. Winning the argument becomes each person's goal.

If we recorded the meeting and then analyzed it, we would find that very few team members ask each other questions. And when they do, the questions are often rhetorical rather than exploratory.

By using discrepancy questions, we can take a vastly different approach during these meetings that can change the team's orientation from *point-counterpoint* to a *collective thought process*. The basic discrepancy question we can ask is this: "*How are we to understand the difference between these points of view?*"

Rather than fight about who is right and who is wrong, the group can begin to understand what the discrepancies are and why they exist.

"*Gosh, you and I are seeing this thing so differently. What do you see that I'm not seeing, and what am I seeing that you're not seeing?*"

When the commission becomes mastering the other points of view and then sorting out the discrepancy, people no longer feel the need to uphold their own position. The group is able to join together in a collective exploration of reality.

The discrepancy question is designed to highlight differences of opinions and then to sort them out. Ayn Rand was fond of saying "Check your premises. Contradictions don't exist." She proposed that contradictions were a matter of faulty perception or misinformation, and the path to understanding them was to examine reality with more intellectual rigor.

Ayn Rand concluded that discrepancies are a telltale sign that our fix on reality is incomplete. In our experience, dramatic learning can take place once discrepancies are sorted out. People realize the assumptions they hold that make it hard for them to observe reality more objectively. When we think we know how things are, we don't ask critical questions. We write in the assumptions as if they were true, and this then becomes a bias. Why would we ask a question when we think we know the answer? The assumptions we hold need to be held up to scrutiny. Do they pass the reality test? How do we know what we are assuming is true? Where's the evidence?

Often these assumptions are in the form of urban myths, fanciful stories that make the rounds year after year as if they were true. These stories are fallacious, but people still seem to love spreading them.

Most organizations have their own urban myths. Managers often hold opinions that contradict the facts before their eyes. When this happens, we know that they are not considering reality but their *concepts* of reality.

These urban myths—or, shall we say, *corporate myths*—can be uncovered during the MMOT through the discrepancy question. How are we to understand the difference between the impressions you have and the facts we can see? If the evidence isn't there, then the impression must not be based on truth.

Like the fellow said, "There's nothing like facts to ruin a good story." The corporate myth is a good story. Many managers within a major pharmaceutical company held one such corporate myth. People claimed that the researchers in the lab were not accountable for the same managerial rigor that was being demanded of the rest of the organization. They didn't work a five-day week. And when they were there, they were having wine parties half the time.

It is hard to believe that reasonable adults could believe these stories, but, in fact, they were teeming throughout the company, except, of course, in the lab. During one meeting in which a few managers were retelling the wine-party story, one of the team members said, "My husband works in the lab, and I can assure you, those people work very hard and aren't having wine parties."

Our minds like to sort things out, resolve discrepancies, neutralize differences, and create a sense of order. The easiest way for the mind to do this is to invent theories to explain the facts. One of the disciplines we need to develop as managers is to understand the difference between fact and theory, exploration and speculation, hard data and conjecture.

There are holes in our understanding of any situation. There always will be. Since our natural tendency is to fill the holes with presumption, we need to become clear about what we base our conclusions on and what biases we build into our thought process. One tool in that exploration is the discrepancy question.

Questions

Questions are a vital part of our managerial discipline. The function of questions is to pursue information, understanding, insight, knowledge, statistics, facts, the essentials of a story. When managers begin to use questions as part of their style, they open up a new world for themselves. When a manager asks a critical question designed to better understand a process, a decision, a policy, an event, or a system, she becomes a guide for a meticulous thought process. At first, the probe is not always welcomed. People may want to avoid what may seem to them as interference. Here's a typical example of an MMOT organically generated by a situation in which the person is avoiding answering direct questions:

"Are we good for the Benson contract?"
"I've got it handled."
"What about the term sheet? Did they agree?"
"Like I said, I've got it handled."
"So they did agree?"
"No, not yet. But we're in good shape, so relax."

This exchange can be titled "Stay Out of My Kitchen." The manager asking the questions is cast in the role of a waiter quizzing the chef on how the soufflé is going. The chef's response is to order the waiter out of the kitchen.

Here is the same conversation as above, but this time with the actual subtext.

"Are we good for the Benson contract?"
"I've got it handled." (Stay out of my business.)
"What about the term sheet? Did they agree?"
"Like I said, I've got it handled." (Stay out of my business.)
"So they did agree?"
"No, not yet. But we're in good shape, so relax." (Stay out of my business.)

The above conversation leads to an MMOT:

"You know, we need to have an MMOT. In reality, I am accountable for the final outcome of this contracting process. Right?" (Information question)
"Right."
"And when I ask you questions to see where we are, you seem to be implying that I shouldn't be asking these questions. Is that what you think?" (Implication question)
"No, I just think that you don't trust me to get the contract signed."
"How so?" (Information question)
"Because you need to check up on my work."
"Part of my job is to track the progress we are making. How can I track it if I don't have real data?" (Information question)
"You want me to update you?"
"Yes, please. And the real issue is this: I ask questions to track how we are doing. Do we need to change our approach? Will your part coordinate with the parts others are doing? Do you see that?" (Information question)
"Yes."
"So reality seems to be this: I ask questions as part of my managerial style, but you thought that it meant I didn't trust you to do the job. Is that a fair statement of what's been happening?" (Information question)
"I think it says it. Yes."

"What are you seeing from this?" (Information question)

"That I've been defensive because I assumed that you had a trust issue with me."

"And now that we've looked at it?" (Information question)

"You just want to stay in touch with what's going on, and asking a lot of questions is how you do that."

"That's right. When I ask questions it's not a statement about trust, it is just my way of keeping everything on track. Sometimes it helps us all reconsider how we are implementing our plans or what has changed that may force us to rethink our plans."

"I see that."

"So the next time I ask you a lot of questions, what will you understand that to mean?" (Information question)

"You are trying to stay on top of everything."

"Right. That's it."

"Yeah, okay, I really see that."

"Great. So how's it coming with the Benson contract?" (Information question)

When rigorous questioning becomes part of the organizational environment, managers begin to learn, explore, study, and grow. Like the MMOT itself, the context of asking each other questions is an acquired taste. But once the managers acquire it, they are able to root their management approach in a solid foundation.

Questions are a powerful tool for true dialogue and exploration. They enable us to see far beyond our usual vantage point. They guide us through new territories. They open new worlds of possibilities. They are the keys to the MMOT.

8

Case Study: The Repeat Offender

Some MMOTs involve a more pronounced confrontation than we have portrayed previously. Consider the following example between Dave and his manager, Terry. Dave has had a work pattern that produces inconsistent work. Often he delivers reports filled with substantive mistakes. Terry and others have tried to correct Dave's pattern, but Dave has never taken these corrections to heart. He always apologizes profusely, blames others, and promises to do better next time. In the following case study, Terry is using the actual MMOT technique with Dave for the first time. Before this, changes were always suggested on the behavioral level: do more of this, do less of that, and so on. Dave has a chronic pattern of casting himself in the role of victim of circumstances. He also tries to get others, especially those who are trying to help him improve, to take on his accountability. He is a talented member of the organization, but his general orientation limits his effectiveness.

Terry is not really being confrontational; rather, he is being honest and objective. Nevertheless, the news is hard for Dave to take. Over the course of the MMOT, part of Terry's job is to enable Dave to become more objective and less subjective. We will see Terry work with each step of the process and, when necessary, go back to a previous step when Dave seems to fall back into his old patterns.

An important report that has just been published and distributed contains four critical mistakes. These are not simple typos, but incorrect data. The report is used to determine policy and make critical strategic decisions. The consequences of decisions based on these errors could be profound.

Terry has just received the report and spotted the mistakes. So have others within senior management—the target audience for the report. In the past Terry has tried different approaches with Dave from being "understanding" to "calling him on the carpet." No matter what the style, the outcome has always been the same: short-term improvement before Dave falls back into the pattern.

In this case study, the long-term impact was real and lasting. Dave became a better manager and learned to perform consistently well. The difference between a simple reprimand and the MMOT was that Terry was able to uncover the critical flaw in Dave's approach and thought process. The following is the first MMOT meeting between Dave and Terry. Many follow-up meetings reinforced the basic conclusions of the first.

STEP ONE: ACKNOWLEDGE REALITY

TERRY

"The reason I wanted to talk to you today is that it turns out that there were four mistakes in the report that we just sent out."

DAVE

"There were? Gosh, I didn't think there were any."

TERRY

"Yeah, it turns out there were four mistakes." [Terry hands Dave a copy of the report with tabs on the pages where there were mistakes. Dave studies the report for a few minutes.]

DAVE

"Oh, sorry. I didn't know—"

TERRY

"Well, this seems to be a pattern."

DAVE

"What do you mean?"

TERRY

"This is not the first time we ended up sending out reports and other materials that had mistakes. Is that true?"

DAVE

"Uh, I guess so. I'm really sorry. This makes me feel awful."

Dave is deflecting reality by addressing how he feels. His assumption is that if he feels badly enough about the situation, he has taken responsibility for it. Terry understands that how he feels is not related to how well he is acknowledging reality. Notice how he acknowledges how Dave feels, but then continues to pursue acknowledging the state of the report and the pattern of mistakes of which this is one example.

TERRY

"I know you're sorry. Would it be correct to say that this is not the first time mistakes have been in the work you are responsible for?"

DAVE

"Yes, but that's because of Al. I've told you that Al is my weak link— that and I need more people."

Dave has shifted from how awful he feels to who is to blame. Notice how Terry does not fall into the trap of talking about how the situation got to be that way. Instead, he continues to establish step one: acknowledge reality.

TERRY

"Tell you what: we'll talk about how this happened in a moment. Right now, we're just trying to establish the facts. And, am I wrong to say that this and past reports and materials, items you have been accountable for, have been sent out with mistakes? Is that a fact?"

DAVE

"I guess so."

TERRY

"Okay. Now, you are the one accountable for these reports, right?"

DAVE

"Yes. I am. And I feel just terrible. But I need more staff and I need a replacement for Al."

TERRY

"Maybe you do, but what do you make of the fact that I, and many others, spotted the mistakes in this latest report and you didn't?"

DAVE

"I didn't think there were any."

TERRY

"But, as you can see from the copy I just gave you, as it turns out, in reality there were four. How did you happen to miss them? And I'm not trying to bite your head off. I just want us to figure out this pattern. Do you agree that this report has four factual mistakes?"

DAVE

"Yes. I see that now."

TERRY

"Okay. So what happened?"

STEP TWO: ANALYZE DAVE'S MANAGERIAL
THOUGHT PROCESS

DAVE

"I counted on my staff."

TERRY

"You didn't read the report?"

DAVE

"I have a lot on my plate. I glanced over it."

TERRY

"Okay, that's helpful to know. If you had read the report, do you think you would have seen the mistakes the way I and others did?"

DAVE

"I guess so."

TERRY

"Okay. And if you saw these mistakes, what would you have done? How would you have handled it?"

DAVE

"I would have made sure they were fixed before we sent out the report."

TERRY

"Right. So, if you had known, you would have corrected them?"

DAVE

"Yup."

Terry decides to go back to step one for a moment to more deeply establish and acknowledge reality.

TERRY

"Here's a factual summary of reality: There has been a pattern of materials going out with mistakes. You are accountable for that material. Had you known before they were sent out, you would have made sure that those mistakes were fixed before the report was published. Is that right?"

DAVE

"Right."

TERRY

"Do you know why this is a big deal?"

DAVE

"I think I do. It makes the entire department look bad."

TERRY

"That's one thing. This company has committed itself to excellence and so these mistakes are unacceptable. But there's another, even more important dimension to this. People are making critical decisions based on our reports. If they have the wrong data they can't make the right decisions. And there's wrong data in these reports. This hurts the business as well as the organization."

DAVE

"I see that, and I'm very sorry."

Dave has gone back to offering Terry his apology and how badly he feels. This time, Terry uses Dave's response to reestablish the point of the conversation.

TERRY

"Remember, what we're doing is trying to figure out how you thought about this online, the decisions you made, and so on. So what happened?"

DAVE

"It's Al, and I need more people."

TERRY

"The way I'm figuring this out is you said that if you had found the mistakes, you would have fixed them before they went out. And I'm assuming you would have caught them, is that right?"

DAVE

"Yeah."

TERRY

"So let's track your thought process as a manager, because that's where we're going to be able to put in the correction. When you first got this assignment, how did you plan on executing it?"

Notice that Terry bypassed the blame game Dave was offering and instead began a "blow-by-blow" tracking of the story.

DAVE

"Well, I met with my staff and told them about the report. Each person had a specific role, and Al was going to coordinate the whole thing."

TERRY

"Since you have doubts about Al, why did you put him in charge?"

Terry follows up this discrepancy question with other questions until he has a fix on how Dave thought about his process.

DAVE

"I need more staff."

TERRY

"Maybe you do, but you didn't have more staff when you got this assignment. So, why Al?"

DAVE

"Well, that's his job, isn't it?"

TERRY

"When you gave Al the job of putting the report together, did you think that he would do a good job or not such a good job?"

DAVE

"Well, Al is Al. So I had my doubts."

TERRY

"Given you had doubts, how did you plan on managing the process?"

DAVE

"Well, I'm busy all the time. So I figured Al could get us 70 percent of the way, and the last 30 percent could be done by someone else."

TERRY

"How did you see your role?"

DAVE

"I would come in at the end and make sure the report was done."

TERRY

"Who was going to handle the last 30 percent?"

DAVE

"Susan."

TERRY

"What did you tell her?"

DAVE

"I just gave her the role of putting the final touches on the report."

TERRY

"What did she understand that to mean?"

DAVE

"I don't know."

TERRY

"But you actually had something in mind?"

DAVE

"Yes. I wanted her to play cleanup and made sure she finished what I thought Al couldn't."

TERRY

"If Susan had played the role that you wanted her to play, does it seem likely it would have worked?"

DAVE

"What do you mean?"

TERRY

"I mean, if Susan knew that you wanted her to play cleanup for Al,

and that she, therefore, became responsible for making sure the report was
ready, on time, and correct, do you think she would have done that job?
Isn't that why you chose her in the first place?"

DAVE
"Oh, yeah, Susan's great."

Dave's plan seems a little more reasonable than it first did. His idea to
use a combination of Al and Susan together would have worked. However, he didn't let Susan know the job he wanted her to do. We can
begin to see that one of Dave's chronic mistakes is expecting people to
know what he wants them to do, even though he has not adequately
communicated that to them. Terry studies Dave's understanding of his
process by asking an "If you had it to do all over" question.

TERRY
"If you had it to do over again, same set of circumstances, what would
you do to make this thing work?"

DAVE
"Oh, I see a few things. I would have read the report myself and made
sure it was correct. And I would have worked more closely with Susan,
whom I was counting on, to make sure she knew what I wanted."

TERRY
"If you did those things, what would the outcome likely have been?"

DAVE
"We wouldn't be having this talk."

TERRY
"So what did you assume was true that turns out not to be true?"

DAVE
"I assumed that Susan knew what I wanted her to do."

TERRY
"What can you learn from seeing that?"

DAVE
"That I have to be clearer."

TERRY
"Good. Do you think this is something you need to do across the board?"

Terry is beginning to combine steps two and three in that he is both analyzing Dave's current thought process and beginning to collect observations that he and Dave can use when they plan for next time.

DAVE

"I guess it is."

TERRY

"How will you do that?"

DAVE

"What? Be more clear about what I expect? Just tell people."

TERRY

"How will you know that they have understood what you've asked them to do?"

Terry is helping Dave think through his actions by asking him to imagine their consequences. This way, Dave goes further in his understanding of what it might take to be effective than he has done in the past.

DAVE

"I'll put it in writing."

TERRY

"A good way to do that is through follow-up e-mails. 'This is what we said in our last meeting . . .' with all the details and expectations, due dates, and so on. That way, you both have a record of it."

DAVE

"Yeah, good idea."

TERRY

"How else might you know they understand what you expect of them?"

DAVE

"Have them tell me, and adjust their impressions if they don't quite get it."

TERRY

"That should work. What about Al? Does he know what you expect of him?"

DAVE

"Al's a case."

TERRY

"But does he know what you expect of him?"

DAVE

"Probably not."

TERRY

"How do you expect Al to do what you want if he doesn't know what you want?"

DAVE

"Well . . ."

TERRY

"If Al's the wrong guy for the job, we'll consider replacing him. But it's better to give him a chance to improve his performance. His chances go up if he knows what you expect, including quality of work, due dates, et cetera. How can you tell how good he might become if he doesn't have clear direction from you?"

Terry is challenging Dave's evaluation of Al because he has been unclear in letting all of his staff know what he expects, including Al. Terry knows that Al will either come up to speed or not be able to do the job. Before Terry is willing to let Dave replace Al, he wants to give Al a chance to improve. This is similar to how Terry is giving Dave a chance to improve.

DAVE

"I see your point. I'll give it a try."

This next move on Terry's part is to take a stand for Dave by letting him know what it means to be accountable. Terry is demonstrating how to make clear expectations and what role he is willing to take in support of Dave.

TERRY

"Good. Now there is one more thing I need you to understand. When you are accountable for a report, I expect you to make sure it is right. I will

be happy to work with you on thinking through your management strategy, but at the end of the day, it is your job to see to it personally that the job gets done right. Is that clear?"

DAVE

"Perfectly."

TERRY

"Good. As you know, in the past, we've tried to put in corrections, but they haven't worked. So this is a new chance to get it right. And both of us need to be aware that we've tried to correct things in the past. Right?"

DAVE

"Right."

TERRY

"So I need you to take a different tack after this conversation. I'm sure we both want this to work. Are you with me?"

DAVE

"One hundred percent."

TERRY

"Now, when's the next report?"

STEP THREE: CREATE A PLAN

DAVE

"We've got one we have to produce by the first of next month."

TERRY

"How have you thought about it before this conversation?"

DAVE

"About the same way as before."

TERRY

"How will you change your approach?"

DAVE

"I'm going to meet with Al and Susan and put together a new plan. I'll tell them what I expect, I'll tell them about the mistakes in the last report, I'll tell them we need to make this next report up to our quality standards, i.e., no mistakes, the right information, well presented, good and useful graphics, and so on. I'll get involved during the process to check on how it's going, and I'll manage the whole thing a lot more closely. And I'll not only read the final draft, I'll read the report as it develops."

TERRY

"If you take those steps, does it look like you will succeed?"

DAVE

"Yeah."

TERRY

"Good. What I'd like you to do is to write me a memo and send it by e-mail about this meeting. Note the current condition, the outcome we want, and how you are going to manage the process from this point on. Can you have that to me by next Monday?"

DAVE

"Certainly."

TERRY

"Good, that way you and I will have the same expectations, and that's important."

DAVE

"Right. But what about the fact that I need more staff?"

TERRY

"I'll look into that, although, you know, they've told us we can't hire any more people right now. We don't know how effective this new management process might be in creating better results, so, without knowing, it's too soon to talk about new people. The job right now is to make the best use of who you do have, and I'll help you think through how to manage them. Okay? That's the point of this conversation. It's to mentor you, to help you become a more effective manager, and to support you."

DAVE

"Okay."

STEP FOUR: CREATING A FEEDBACK SYSTEM

TERRY

"Now the last thing is that we need a feedback system, so I know how you're doing with these changes. How about we meet next week, and you give me a report to update me. That way, if there are other things you need to do as a manager, we can talk about them."

DAVE

"Yeah."

TERRY

"So please make sure you get on my appointment book and I'll see you next week. And I hope this process helps the way we are working together."

DAVE

"Yeah, thanks. I hope so too."

From that point on, Terry met with Dave for about ten minutes for the next several weeks until the next report was complete. Al and Susan began to work well together, and Dave decided to keep Al in the department. Dave was able to generalize many management lessons from this MMOT, and he went on to become a reliable professional. His orientation changed as well. He no longer saw himself as a victim of circumstances, but as the person who manages to perform well, no matter what the circumstances happen to be. Dave's change was directly related to his understanding of what was making the process he was using not work well, and his ability to master the steps that it would take to produce outstanding performance. Often managers underestimate the importance of what makes a process work or not work. The general assumption is that these matters are so trivial and simple that they do not warrant attention. The reality is quite the opposite. Dave's previous behavior was his way of compensating for his feeling of powerlessness. He didn't know how to manage the process, so he reverted to situational thinking. Once Terry began to mentor him, he began to understand the mechanics of his managerial process. Dave was empowered by truth, support from Terry, and the ability to step back from his subjective reactions. Dave then was able to evaluate reality objectively, including his own weaknesses and strengths, and design a better process over time.

9

Truth Within the Team

Often managerial moments of truth concern how people interact with each other rather than how each individual may have performed. Often teams see themselves as individual solo contributors who happen to be working together, rather than an aligned group of professionals forming a single cohesive entity. The classic line that epitomizes this attitude is: "Your part of the boat is sinking."

In *The Fifth Discipline*, Peter Senge describes what he calls "the myth of the management team." He writes:

> Standing forward to do battle with these dilemmas and disabilities is "the management team," the collection of savvy, experienced managers who represent the organization's different functions and areas of expertise. Together, they are supposed to sort out the complex cross-functional issues that are critical to the organization. . . .
>
> All too often, teams in business tend to spend their time fighting for turf, avoiding anything that will make them look bad personally, and pretending that everyone is behind the team's collective strategy—maintaining the appearance of a cohesive team. To keep up the image, they seek to squelch disagreement; people with serious reservations avoid stating them publicly, and joint decisions are watered-down compromises reflecting what everyone can live with, or else reflecting one person's view foisted on the group. If there is disagree-

ment, it's usually expressed in a manner that lays blame, polarizes opinion, and fails to reveal the underlying differences in assumptions and experience in a way that the team as a whole could learn.

In his usual eloquent fashion, Senge cuts to the chase. Too often, our teams are governed by underlying dynamics that make it difficult for people to truly join forces on behalf of their goals. Too often, teams are not what we want them to be or what they could be. *Yet the team is the most important unit within the organization.* It is through teams that most decisions are made and carried out. If we are able to increase overall team performance throughout the company, the organization becomes dramatically more effective.

Teams usually avoid addressing the numerous moments of truth that occur. People don't want to rock the boat, they want to be supportive, and they fear being disruptive. They want to avoid a "tit-for-tat" pointing out of their mistakes if they happen to mention the mistakes of others. The team's tendency, even more than the individual's, is to avoid conflict. One famous pattern of group dynamics is that people avoid talking about the most controversial or critical issues they face until the very end of the meeting, when the clock has run out. Someone brings up the most important issues only when there's no more time to address them.

But we can change team dynamics. We can create an environment in which people can create synergy, momentum, and a high level of coordination and alignment. Truth telling is the one fundamental that makes building the team possible. Without the practice of telling the truth, not much can change.

For years, management teams have been taken to ropes courses or to the woods or on white-water rafting trips to foster "team building." Once in the wilderness, the team gels. People begin to work together, align with each other, and demonstrate that they are capable of outstanding team performance. But once back in the organization, they revert to their old patterns very quickly. What can we learn by this type of team-building experience? Under the right conditions, the very same people who seemed not to be able to align with each other can come together as a brilliantly performing team. We can also observe that it is not the actual individuals who limit the team's ability to function well. Rather, it is the *organizational context* in which they work. If we can change the context, we can change the team's performance.

What are the common differences between the team's "white-water" and "meeting room" performances?

White-water Team-Building Trip	In the Meeting Room
Clear roles, goals, rules	Unclear roles, goals, rules
Tasks seen in relationship to outcomes	Tasks driven by problems
Managers tell each other the truth	Managers avoid conflict
Managers align resources within the whole context	Managers protect their own resources
Managers sort out conflicts of interest	Managers avoid pointing out conflicts of interest
Managers are willing to explore each other's ideas	Managers advocate their own opinions

MMOT Within the Team

When the team has been introduced to the MMOT technique, it can transform itself. The team can drive its own learning process. Before, people thought they were being open simply because they were stating their opinions or positions. During an MMOT, the team members explore their collective thought process. The first few times thinking through an MMOT can be revelatory. People are able to understand the interrelationships they have with each other and with their environment. They can identify their real conflicts of interest and sort them out. They can coordinate their individual and collective resource base, which is quite different from the usual pattern of protecting their own resources from each other. Any confusion they may have about the outcome they are after can be addressed and sorted out. The team members can look at reality as it is and as it changes. Successes and mistakes both serve as learning experiences that contribute to collective learning, adjustments, and improved performance.

How Does the Team Use the MMOT?

Any manager within the team can lead an MMOT. Often it is the leader, but some of the most powerful and instructive MMOTs come from others. All four steps help the team separate information so that the group can stay on topic more easily. Acknowledging reality (step one) often becomes a collective process of inquiry. What exactly is reality? What evidence do we have? Are we seeing all the essentials? Is the data valid? How do we know? Analyzing the team's thought process (step two) enables the group to step back and see their collective management style from a greater and more objective perspective. Changes in their approach (step three: create a plan) often become obvious and easy to adopt, and the ongoing feedback system (step four) is built into their regular meeting schedule, as everyone now knows how they want to operate and is willing to self-correct as needed.

A large high-tech company's senior executive suggested a cross-functional products team consider introducing a new product line. The team was made up of people from marketing, finance, product development, and sales. The group took on the senior executive's recommendation as if it were their marching orders. They created business cases for the proposed new line, and they went through endless hours of PowerPoint presentations. Every time the team came to a decision point, they would break out into pros and cons. For every pro there was a con, and for every con, a pro. The team was finding it increasingly difficult to reach a decision. The team members described themselves as "spinning their wheels," a frustration that was common before their first MMOT.

After many fruitless meetings, with the frustration level rising each time, someone in the group asked a simple question: "Who is our target customer?" This was such a basic question that it seemed obvious to ask early on in the process. But, as is the case all too often

in very large organizations, the team interpreted the recommendation from the senior executive as an edict, and their job was to see to
it that the product type was introduced. They had engaged in the
process without asking critical questions, understanding the essential
idea behind the new product type, or even knowing the point of the
exercise in which they were involved.

After that question was asked, the team formally began an
MMOT process. The first thing they did was acknowledge their current state, which was: as a group, they didn't have a clear idea of what
they were trying to accomplish. They were embarrassed and surprised that they had based all their work on assumptions that they
now saw as questionable. They described that event of asking "Who
is the target customer?" as an "emperor has no clothes" moment.
They looked around the room in stunned silence, and then a few
people started to chuckle. A light had turned on. They had seen a
pattern they had lived through many times in the past. Now they had
come to understand that they were acting without real understanding. They talked about this as the critical moment of truth for the
team, one that changed their performance patterns and professional
relationships with one another.

The team readily acknowledged the current situation, including its
lack of understanding and the resulting "wheel spinning." They asked
themselves questions to track the process that led them to this point.
From that, they began to articulate the various assumptions team
members had written into their thought processes. Many of these assumptions were not true, and others were true but incomplete.

They also saw that they were trying to organize themselves from the
"inside out" rather than from the "outside in," as one team member described it. Before their MMOT, they were acting in a vacuum, isolated
from marketplace realities, ignoring the competition, following what
they assumed were orders. They realized the original suggestion was
just that: a suggestion, not an order. In fact, the senior executive had
tried to be helpful in making the recommendation and didn't realize the
team had taken it as a deliverable it felt compelled to accomplish. The
team saw that it could be subject to groupthink, and that team members
needed to change the fundamentals of how they were operating.

Then they began to answer the original question: Who is the target customer? They took the question seriously, and in the next meeting, they examined relevant data that filled in the picture. They analyzed how large the opportunity was and if the company was capable of competing. They saw that they had not been effective in penetrating the type of market they were considering entering. They studied their competition. They studied themselves more honestly and objectively than they had ever attempted before.

The group transformed itself from one that avoided difficult decisions, talked at each other, engaged in chronic speculation, and steered clear of self-criticism to a team that cut off hypothesizing quickly in favor of real data, questioned each other more freely as a real exploration, sought clarity where needed, and engaged in a collective thought process. Once ideas were brought to the task stage, the team was able to perform effectively because the members could be candid with one another.

The team's MMOT changed it dramatically. The members rethought the senior executive's suggestion and decided it was a good one. They asked themselves tough questions. Once they saw how much more capable the competition seemed to be than they were, they asked themselves, "What's wrong with us, then?" They drove for real understanding, and their insights enabled them to become more disciplined and more effective. In the end, they did successfully enter the new line of business.

Often the obvious is hard to see until the team *collectively* explores reality together. One or two people having insights that prove to be accurate won't help the team until everyone studies reality together and can understand these insights. Before that, the team can only trade opinions, which leads to people staking out territory rather than engaging in a true group inquiry process.

The Senior Executive Team and the MMOT

Such efforts are not limited to project or product teams. Every team in the organization, right up to the most senior executive team, can benefit from facing managerial moments of truth.

In a way, most executive teams are not management teams as such, in that each senior executive is a leader of her department, function, or discipline. The executive team is in charge of overall strategic planning and the implementation of those plans, but these people do not actually work together as closely as many other teams throughout the organizational system. Nonetheless, their need to face managerial moments of truth is even more critical to the health and well-being of the business and the organization.

Many executive teams feel that facing these issues is "tactical" rather than "strategic." By labeling confronting reality as "tactical," the team can avoid sorting through many of the thornier challenges it has, including issues around the distribution of power and authority, accountability, and executive team performance as a whole. Too often, executives on the most senior levels want to protect their positions and their careers. Then the organization's driving vision becomes watered down as it is translated to the rest of the organization through the filter of internal competing interests from the top.

Senior-team MMOTs are often the most difficult and the most important if an organization is to operate at a level of candor in the service of building a great company. Jim Collins speaks eloquently in *Good to Great* about the importance of creating a vision that people are passionate about. Great management emerges from both heart and mind. In Collins's 2005 *Fortune* article, "How to Make Great Decisions," he points out that the best decisions arise from candid, indeed, passionate debate in a senior team. Our experience is that the presence of that debate often comes in the form of the MMOT. It is one team member telling it like it is in regard to past, present, or future commitments that must be made for the organization to achieve superior performance. That can come in the form of a question. Why didn't we achieve our sales goal? Did we set the goal with good information on the market? Did we allocate resources to achieve it? And so on.

These questions are, of course, step two in the MMOT—preceded by step one—and if faithfully followed will yield to steps three and four so performance improves. This team MMOT isn't easy.

Public acknowledgment of the need to improve can quickly feel personal and prevent us from getting to the unvarnished truth and making the necessary corrections.

To the extent a team can't have these types of discussions, real learning and real improvement cannot occur. Socrates taught us that from inquiry, debate, and dialogue new truths emerge. And the truths that happen in a senior management setting can indeed set it free—free to take responsibility for making change happen and holding each other accountable for performance. As with a personal MMOT, team MMOTs create a format for bringing disagreements and performance issues to the table before they fester. They give the team a chance to make corrections before performance can't be recovered. And this needs to happen irrespective of title or responsibility. Leaving titles at the door is, practically speaking, impossible. However, if the team believes passionately in the importance of the enterprise's mission, it will trust that truth telling isn't bounded by rank. In fact, any top manager wants the truth on the table so she can deal with it. Teams that don't have experience in MMOT should start slowly using the technique to take the sting out of candor. Blue Shield managers often say "I need to have a moment of truth with you" as a way of acknowledging this is about learning, rather than about putting a team member on the spot.

Finally, using the MMOT in senior teams (or anywhere else, for that matter) should be saved for reasonably important lapses in performance. Knowing when to use or not use MMOT isn't driven by a formula. We all know that using it to deal with someone being two minutes late to a meeting is overkill. However, there is no neon sign on behavior that says, "Use MMOT now!" This is where managers earn their money, by using their judgment to apply MMOT to the right situation. Given that we are naturally averse to conflict, we should initially err on the side of using it more than less.

This is consistent with the overall strategy of addressing managerial moments of truth early in the process rather than letting them develop. The additional insight here is to pick those behaviors that really matter to organizational performance. In the end, it is a managerial judgment call that relies on clearly assessing the importance of changing a person's performance pattern.

A prime example of truth telling on the executive level comes from Tom Flanagan, president and COO of BMO (Bank of Montreal) InvestorLine, Canada's leading discount brokerage. For the past five years, BMO's InvestorLine has been ranked as *the* top online brokerage firm by Gomez Canada and *The Globe and Mail*, and Flanagan as one of the country's leading business leaders. Flanagan describes how truth telling within the senior team has led to InvestorLine's success:

> Very early on in developing the team within BMO InvestorLine we recognized that we had tremendous strengths in the leaders of our functional areas. We would continue to advance our development efforts and move the firm forward in the very competitive discount brokerage industry in Canada. We were continually looking for ways in which we could find the *one* product, the *one* service that would revolutionize the way discount brokerage was offered and create our differentiated product offering.
>
> There was a realization that with the pace of change in online brokerage, and with the creative juices working overtime within all of our competitors, the pursuit of a competitive magic bullet was unlikely.
>
> Instead, we began to work at building a *true* executive team within the organization and [to] narrow our focus on what the match is between our products and services to the client's needs. There was a fundamental change within the organization when we began to better appreciate that everything is interconnected with everything else, *and we had to become brutally honest with what we could accomplish and what required additional study.*
>
> Truly coordinating each of the functional units so that each executive is forthcoming with their ideas and enabling an environment where other functional executives challenge for greater clarity is a continuous work in progress. Truly communicating at a creative discussion level has been instrumental in moving the BMO InvestorLine management team and the organization to our current levels of success.
>
> We need to continuously remind everyone that each of their agen-

das needs to fit within the strategic intent of the firm. There are a lot of fun things happening with the online brokerage marketplace and some real nifty technologies, products, services, and marketing ideas. We simply remind each other on a continuous basis, both individually and collectively, that some creative ideas take us on a tangent away from our core strategy. We need to remain focused on our goals.

Achieving a level of team interaction that thrives on discussion and putting our cards on the table for the collective performance of the organization is not always easy. It requires an approach by everyone that may be more like the openness and honesty we expect from our family.

What is interesting about BMO's InvestorLine path to the consistent success it enjoys is the truth factor. Yet, telling the truth and disciplining the team to focus on their core strategy does not stifle creativity or inventiveness. If anything, the "brutal honesty" focuses their collective creative juices and their high level of performance.

Facing Truth in Light of Success

We invited William Brandt, the cofounder and former CEO of American Woodmark, a company that makes kitchen cabinets, to write the following piece about the challenges of facing reality when times are good and people are feeling pride in their performance and in their past decisions. It takes a wise executive team not to be fooled by its own good press and to look at reality more critically when everyone else is celebrating your triumphs.

In the following account, Brandt is not describing a formal MMOT process but talks cogently about how truth telling within the context of his company's long-term strategy enabled people to change some of the basic organizing principles of their business.

The American Woodmark Story
William Brandt
Change is difficult at any time, but it is most difficult when times are going well. By every financial or competitive measure, American

Woodmark was a very successful company in 1989. We were experiencing record sales and earnings and had become the leading supplier of stock kitchen cabinets to the home-center industry. This success, however, masked a much darker reality, one that we did not want to acknowledge because it had no apparent resolution. As the CEO I came to realize that our current strategy would lead to the company's ruin if continued unchecked into the 1990s. We had grown along with our home-center accounts as they expanded from local to regional service areas. This was great initially, since we had no other customers in their respective regions. By the late 1980s, however, our major home-center accounts, such as the Home Depot, were expanding nationally and entering markets that we had long serviced with independent distributors. Where this happened, we experienced an immediate conflict with our distributors, who had previously enjoyed an exclusive representation. Furthermore, the home centers also entered each other's geographical regions and began competing directly with one another. Faced with this new competition, both distributors and home centers responded by looking for additional or replacement stock cabinet lines to sell. I could see that the conflicts we were then experiencing would only intensify as time went on, leading to even greater customer dissatisfaction and eventual lost sales.

Our first step was to acknowledge this reality, and the second was to analyze it and consider its implications. Once this situation was apparent to me, it took another six months of discussion for our senior management team to reach a common understanding of our reality. After much soul searching we concluded that our only hope to remain a viable company was to radically restructure our business, tearing down many of the strategic assets we had spent the better part of a decade creating.

Our third step was to create a new strategy which we called our "1995 Vision." The key elements of this vision were as follows:

- *multiple brands*—expand from a single brand to separate brands with unique product styles for independent distributors and key home-center accounts;

- *product variety*—expand the number of unique styles from eighteen to over one hundred;
- *just-in-time manufacturing*—shut down eleven regional distribution centers and ship all orders within the same lead times from three regional assembly plants.

We anticipated that it would take us six years to fully implement this vision.

The organization's reaction to this new direction was quite mixed. Our sales and marketing people, who had lived with the frustration of their customers over market conflicts, were ecstatic that we were taking action to correct this situation. Additional brands and product lines would give them much more to sell. Our manufacturing and logistics people, however, were almost in a state of shock. They could not understand why we would attempt to change so radically when things were going apparently so well.

Our fourth step, the implementation of the plan, anticipated a series of action steps spaced out over the six-year period. We projected overall slow growth in sales and profits, compared to our experience of dramatic growth during the 1980s. The six-year horizon I thought would provide us the necessary time to accomplish an orderly transition.

By 1991 we had established a separate brand of cabinets for independent distributors and had expanded our product offering to forty-five styles. Our manufacturing and logistic operations were bogged down in their transitions and were looking for a chance to digest the changes made to date. Therefore, we planned for only a few new styles that year. Early in the year, however, we experienced a sudden shock to our business. Our two largest home-center accounts informed us that they had decided to add a second core supplier of stock cabinets. We faced the possibility of losing 50 percent or more of our volume with each account. The primary factor for this decision was the increasing conflict with the "American Woodmark" brand at competing home centers.

This period became a true moment of truth in the life of our company. At a historic meeting our senior management resolved to do whatever was necessary to regain the confidence and meet the needs of our key home-center and distributor customers and to do so as rapidly as possible. Out of this resolve came the commitment to create a separate brand for one of the two home centers and to complete the product expansion to over one hundred styles, both in time for a spring 1992 kitchen and bath show introduction. The entire organization put its energy into this initiative. Everyone now understood the magnitude of our deteriorating market position. We expanded factories to accommodate the new lines; incurred huge marketing, product development, and manufacturing start-up costs; continued the gradual elimination of distribution centers; and absorbed significant losses for the year.

At the kitchen and bath show the following spring, the impact was dramatic. The separate home-center brand reduced conflict among all home centers, and updated product styles for all home-center and distributor accounts enabled us to refurbish displays and generate excitement at the retail level.

It took us from 1993 to 1996 to complete the implementation of the 1995 Vision. We rationalized our manufacturing processes to support a just-in-time production environment and completed the phase-out of distribution centers. Our journey did not follow the relatively straight and safe path I had projected in 1989. It took us longer than expected to get there, and we got severely bruised along the way.

Although it was a difficult transition, we were successful in achieving all of the major strategic elements of the 1995 Vision. We expanded our brand offering from one to three lines and increased the product styles offered fivefold. We became a product development leader where we had been a follower. With our just-in-time manufacturing orientation we eliminated eleven distribution centers, reducing finished goods inventory by more than tenfold. Even without the distribution centers, our delivery times remained constant. We regained the confidence of our customers and reestablished our leadership position in the stock segment of the home-center industry. The strategic platform established has been the basis for the company's rapid growth from 1995 to the present. Currently American Wood-mark competes with strong brands in each of the market segments it serves.

Now, moments of truth are the defining elements of our culture. We have incorporated tools for understanding and communicating current reality into the company's management processes. We realize that one of our strongest competitive advantages we have is in our ability to tell the truth, call it like it is, deal with it productively, learn from it, implement that learning, and continually study the impact we are creating.

The Truth-Telling Team

The MMOT within the context of the team is based on a premise of truth telling. Truth telling, as we have said, is not a matter of each person stating his opinion and then holding to his own position. Rather, it is matter of the team making it its business to find out how reality actually is and explore each other's vantage points. At first, this is hard to do. It becomes easier with practice and experience. It becomes possible when the team insists that truth be told, whatever it is.

Teams gel when members can tell each other the truth. When they can't, people adopt civil behavior, try to perform well under limited circumstances, and pretend that reality is different from how everyone knows it is. The famous "elephant in the room" that no one will talk about is a clever metaphor that illustrates the human tendency to bend over backwards to avoid the conflict we may feel if we confront reality. If there is an elephant in the room, everyone knows it, and if they can't see it, they certainly can smell it. The group decision to not mention it undermines the group's effectiveness. It takes resolve for us to change the pattern. It manifests in a variety of ways. For some it takes courage; for others, clarity about their professional purpose, dedication to the objective truth, or a highly practical wisdom that comes from knowing that nothing less than the truth can lead us to exceptional performance.

10
Managing the Mismatch

Occasionally an MMOT reveals that there is a *mismatch* between the individual and the role he is playing. The mismatch may concern the values or the mission of the organization, the skills or competence required to do the job, or the employee's attitude, alignment, or interests.

When there is a mismatch, and it is not changeable in an acceptable amount of time, the person must leave the position or the organization. We prefer that that course of action be the last resort. The MMOT gives us a chance to save the situation if we can.

The Great Performer with Bad Attitude

We all know them, the people who perform miracles, pull rabbits out of their hats, drive up sales, drive down costs, make their aggressive due dates, contribute to the bottom line, increase market share, invent new products, and walk on water. The only thing is, they leave "dead bodies" in their wake.

Through the MMOT, these people may come around, transform themselves, and continue to be great contributors to the organization, but now with a new user-friendly approach that everyone welcomes. Too often, though, this type of high performer with a bad attitude is a prima donna, lording it over everyone. These people think they have immunity from common rules of behavior because their bad manners or heavy-handed ways are offset by their great performance.

One such person was Pete, a director of manufacturing for a company that produced industrial cleaning products. He was a master at calculating manufacturing cost structures, updating computerization for streamlining processes, redeploying shipping and warehousing methods, and increasing manufacturing efficiency. However, he was exceedingly disruptive within the organization. He regularly tried to lead "palace revolts" against senior management. He treated his direct reports unfairly, engaged in gossip, hollered at people on the line, and created problems with the union leadership.

The organization was afraid to let him go because he was the only person within the company who deeply understood its unique manufacturing processes. He had saved the company a tremendous amount of money, increased its production capacity, and given it an exceptional competitive advantage. The company had invested a great deal of time and money in Pete in the form of training, consultants, and management coaches.

If the company had to replace Pete, it would fall well behind its production schedule because of the time it would take to bring a new person up to speed. Pete didn't have a solid second in command in his organization, so no one could quickly take over.

Pete knew he had the company over a barrel. He ignored all the pleas and threats from people trying to improve the situation. He knew that he was safe and didn't have to listen.

HOLDING THE COMPANY HOSTAGE

Like too many highly valued performers with bad attitudes, Pete was holding the company hostage.

People like Pete undermine the organization's ability to develop their management teams. It takes great clarity, resolve, and sense of long-range building of the capacity of the organization to face reality and confront the situation.

Organizations often avoid a managerial moment of truth in these cases. No one wants to be the one who put production behind, or lost the big account, or slowed down sales because she fired a mismatched problem child. The Petes of the world know the game, and they learn where the line is between enough redeemable value and harm to the organization.

Over time, any management initiatives to align the team, or develop better systems, or redistribute power and authority are thwarted. The Petes do not want alternatives that will make it easier to replace them.

Do they know the game they are playing? To some degree, yes. Is there a chance they can change? Yes. But the company must be willing to suffer some temporary setbacks on the way to a healthier organization, because it may have to let this person go.

It is impossible to have an MMOT with a Pete type unless we are willing to let this person go. Without that consequence, not much can change. This is because by the time we would address this situation the person already has been talked to, cajoled, reasoned with, humored, threatened, coached, consulted, confronted, sent to leadership courses, sent to managerial charm school, and given the best chance anyone could ever get.

So we need to take two critical steps before we decide to conduct an MMOT with a Pete:

- We need to be in a situation in which if the Pete type did leave, the damage would be manageable; in other words, we want to pick the right time for our battle.
- We need to be willing to let the Pete type go. If we are not willing to fire him, we won't get his attention.

The MMOT with the Problem Child

Once we are willing to face reality, we need to set the stage. How will we operate if our Pete is gone? We need to consider the logistics, the critical areas we need to cover, the security codes we need to get into the computer, and anything else that might make our life hard if the person leaves.

We need to document the situation. Check with HR to understand the company's legal obligations and risks. Make sure that we
have given this person ample and accurate, honest feedback over
time. We need to play a fair game.

We hope the person is redeemable. We have invested much in this
person, and the best outcome is that he stays but improves. To have a
chance to reach this goal, we must be willing and prepared to let the
person go. Nothing short of this will be effective.

The actual Pete of this example did go through an MMOT. Senior
management decided to face the situation and take whatever measures
necessary. They prepared the groundwork and then called Pete in.
They let him know that the agenda of the meeting was his management
style. They made sure that he wasn't ambushed or treated unfairly.

ACKNOWLEDGE REALITY

Pete met with two of his senior managers. They scheduled
enough time to address the issues adequately. They introduced the
subject by saying:

*"You know, we've had a lot of trouble with your management style, and
we are here today to address it. Now, before we begin to look at this issue,
we need you to know that this issue is important enough for us to decide
whether you continue in the organization or not."*

Without knowing the stakes, Pete would have been disadvantaged in
understanding the seriousness of the meeting and the behaviors they
were addressing.

Pete's managers told him:

*"Even though you are a valued member of the organization, and your
performance has always been outstanding, your managerial style is unacceptable. It is disruptive. People don't want to work for you. You have mis-
represented us to the union, and that's made things harder than they
should be. We are ready to cite examples of this behavior, but I know you've
heard this type of criticism before. This is not news to you, is it?"*

Pete agreed that it was not news, but then he became defensive, blaming others for his own behavior, presenting himself as misunderstood.

"Do you agree with the criticism?"

"No."

"Why not?"

"They shouldn't be picking on me. Without me, the company would be in trouble."

"We are looking at reality. Is it true that you have been disruptive?"

"I should be getting a raise given all I do."

"We both have decisions to make. Should we be trying to improve your management style or should we just part ways?"

"Well, it's inconvenient for me to have to find another job right now."

"That's no reason to stay. Do you get that people around here label you a troublemaker?"

"I think I've heard that."

"Why do you think they say that?"

"I don't know."

"Have you ever asked them?"

"No."

"Do you want to know why?"

"Yes."

At first Pete begrudgingly admitted his impact on others. The question his senior managers asked repeatedly was why others had that impression of him. They went over reality carefully, objectively, and truthfully.

Finally Pete came to a moment of truth for himself. Did he want to be in the organization or not? He saw that this MMOT wasn't going away, and he had one of two choices: he could hide from reality or face it. His senior managers were offering him a chance to change his ways. It was up to him.

The meeting was hard for everyone. But the senior managers had resolved that the values of the organization, which included how people were treated, were more important than any individual, no matter how valuable he was to the company.

The message from management was an ultimatum: change or leave. But the attitude of the senior managers was not to pressure Pete into good behavior, because that change would be only a temporary reaction to the pressure they were exerting. They were offering him a new chance to rethink his approach, align with the organization's values, and be involved with the company as a true team player.

Pete didn't like reality, but after awhile he admitted that he was using his value as a performer to justify his disruptive behavior. Before he was able to see that, he talked about all he had done for the company and his unique contribution, for which he felt unappreciated.

After forty minutes of stating reality, exploring every objection Pete had to the reports, and after Pete was forced to see that, in reality, he was abusing his role in the company, he changed the way he was listening. He became more objective, and partly this was because the senior managers were not out to get him, but out to change the temperament of the organization.

Pete finally saw that reality was, indeed, that he was using his success to excuse bad behavior. He decided to stay and change his ways.

His choice was based on tracking how he made his managerial decisions (step two of the MMOT technique). Time and again, as each situation was analyzed, Pete began to see his pattern. Often his worst behavior came right after big triumphs. His general attitude was explored from the vantage point of his orientation, in which he felt like an unappreciated hero.

Pete created a plan for change. The senior managers asked him if he wanted another coach to help him through the process. He admitted that he had not taken past coaches seriously; he would pay lip service to their suggestions but wait for them to fail so he could get rid of them. He asked to try to improve his manner without help, and, only if he couldn't do it, to ask for help. The senior managers agreed and set up a timetable. They wanted to see continuous improvement in his behavior—not a dramatic change followed by regression to his old ways. They set up a succession plan in case it didn't work out. Part of Pete's job was to train others in what he knew, to have capable people around him, to create a manual for every system he ran, and to have the systems tested by other people running them for periods of time.

Pete had, in fact, a real moment of truth with himself, and he made a fundamental choice to change. This event was literally a day of reckoning that forced Pete to face the way he lived.

A fundamental choice is one that is about state of being, orientation, and resolve. If you've never made the fundamental choice to be a nonsmoker, any approach you try to quit smoking will not work long-term. If you have made the fundamental choice to be a nonsmoker, then any method you choose will work and you will especially be attracted to those approaches that work best for you.

That's what happened to Pete. But it is only because of facing a critical MMOT that he was motivated to change.

And change he did. Over the next few years, Pete became one of the best leaders and managers within the organization. A few years after his MMOT, he was asked to lead management workshops within the organization, and he became one of the most respected members of the company.

One Blue Shield of California manager talked about a mismatch that led to a parting of the ways:

I had a team member who was technically very strong, but was a bull in a china shop when it came to interpersonal skills. He was very bright and competent in his field but did not believe the how was as important as the what. He was not collaborative in his working relationships and did not do well in team efforts. While I knew this was a problem, I probably waited too long to start dealing with the behaviors. The final straw was when a key partner approached me and very directly told me that they had a vote of no confidence in this person. I had a major moment of truth with this person and laid out the specifics—citing examples of performance feedback, peer feedback, and results. At the time we were rolling out new leadership principles and spent time discussing what they meant. We then prepared a performance improvement plan that described specific behaviors that would be evident when our new leadership principles were being practiced. We talked about personal fit with the culture. The person needed time to digest all of this. He came back a week later and said that he did not think he was the right fit for the culture and resigned from the position. He was unwilling to change his ends-justifies-the-means approach, and he understood that there wasn't a match between his management style and our organizational values and leadership principles.

Good managers must be sensitive to this pattern and confront it early on. As this manager states, he should have gotten involved sooner in dealing with this person. But most managers would do the very same thing: not address behavior issues until the problem becomes extreme, particularly if the person in question is an accomplished performer you rely on. If we get into the habit of identifying the managerial moment of truth and addressing it early on, we up our chances of successfully integrating a person who needs an attitude makeover.

THE FACTORS THAT NEED TO MATCH
Four distinct factors need to match: skill, attitude, alignment, and interest.

Any factor that is inadequate creates a mismatch. Can we enable a manager to move from a mismatch to a match? That will always be the question when one or more of these factors are missing from the mix.

COMBINATIONS
Skill, attitude, alignment are in place, but interest is missing.

One senior executive had this very combination. He was a very capable professional, wonderful attitude, was deeply aligned with the mission and values of the organization, and yet his role was not of interest to him. He had played that role in the past, and his feeling was "been there, done that." At first it was hard for him and the others on the senior team to identify just where the mismatch was. He performed well; he was a valued leader in the organization, and the people who worked for him liked him and his management style. But something was missing. When the organization grew, his position became more demanding. This made the mismatch more pronounced, because he tried his best to become enthusiastic about his newly expanded role, but his heart just wasn't in it.

He had an MMOT with his boss. While they were exploring reality, he suddenly realized that he wasn't interested in playing the role he would need to play. He could do it, he had the right attitude, he was aligned, but he was not interested in the work he was commissioned to do.

From this discovery, he and his boss tried to find a role for him within the organization that would interest him. He created a temporary position for himself as a transition while he and his boss considered what role he might play in the future. As it turned out, there wasn't a role that would have satisfied his professional interest, and eventually he left the company under the most favorable circumstances.

Without understanding the "interest factor," he may have stayed longer, and the mismatch would have taken longer to understand. Mismatches that are not understood often have a way of revealing themselves in less productive ways than did the manager in this story.

Skill, attitude, interest are in place, but alignment is missing.

Alignment is not agreement, and it is important not to confuse the two. We can be aligned to the mission, values, and the strategy of the organization, yet debate policies or decisions that are proposed.

On the other hand, managers can agree with one another about the actions they need to take and yet not be aligned with the overall governing principles of the company.

Aligned managers understand how important it is to test ideas, foster due diligence in investigating data, explore assumptions, and ask pointed questions to reach better outcomes. But they also under-stand that the context of alignment means that they are working to-ward the same ends, moving in the same direction, joining together to bring out the best in the group and in themselves, and focusing on the success of the enterprise.

Questions of alignment have had a negative impact on many large organizations. For example, in the old days of Digital Equipment (late 1970s to early 1980s) alignment was missing in action. Any new idea that a manager proposed had to survive aggressive and mean-spirited pounding from the team of engineers assigned to support it. The notion was that if an idea could withstand this type of tough punishment, it must be okay.

However, those ideas that made it through weren't always the best ones. Rather, the personality of the idea's owner or the forcefulness of the defense enabled an idea to outlive the ordeal, even though the idea itself was questionable. The harder managers had to fight to get heard, the more out of alignment the groups were, and the more mismatches there were all around the organization.

Alignment is a requisite for the organization. Without it, man-agers pull in different directions. With it, managers have an overall organizing principle that motivates them to pull together.

It's not always easy to put your finger on just what alignment is. Everyone claims that he is aligned. Often, the spirit of alignment is more tangible than any event or pattern of behavior. When people are aligned, they act in good faith, they root for the organization's success, they roll up their sleeves and dedicate themselves to the cause, and they care about the organization.

When alignment is missing, often the manager leading the MMOT must help the person question his commitment to the work of the organization.

Managers rarely think to ask for alignment. But often people are more than happy to align with the project, idea, values, mission, and the higher purpose of their organizations. The thought never oc-curred to them, and no one had asked them before. The only time it is hard for a manager to align with her organization is when the organization is acting in ways that are contradictory to the person's values, or there is a conflict of interest, or the person does not want to support the aims of the company.

If achieving alignment is not possible, the person may support the organization by his professional services rendered, but this person shouldn't be burdened with a leadership role for which alignment is critical.

Skill, interest, and alignment are in place, but attitude is missing.

Not all unacceptable attitudes are overtly disruptive. Sometimes the mismatch between the organization and the manager is found in a subtle cynicism, or a quietly undermining put-down, or in a joke that is designed to criticize and challenge the work that everyone is doing. These types of actions are hard to point out, because they are so small, and it seems petty to put them under the microscope. However, when a manager chronically demonstrates these types of behaviors, we have an attitude issue.

When having an MMOT with such a person, it is important to contrast how he has acted in meetings with how you want him to act. The point of an MMOT is truth. Often, the person will not know he is acting in ways that put his attitude in question. At first the person will claim it's only his personality. We are not in the business of changing people's personalities, but we can ask for professional support, which may require adjusting how someone behaves around the organization.

The personality defense was used when sexual harassment issues first arose in the organization. But organizations needed to teach managers that they needed to change any offensive behavior, personality idiosyncrasy notwithstanding.

If there is an attitude mismatch, the MMOT will concern adjustments on the level of attitude, which is a fair requirement within the managerial professional demands of the organization.

Interest, attitude, and alignment are in place, but skill is missing.

This is a good person, one who does his best but somehow doesn't cut it. We often assume that the person has the skills to do the job.

How else would he have made it this far in the organization? Too often, however, a good person simply doesn't have the needed skills. Perhaps he has been promoted beyond his skill level.

This MMOT concerns the question of acquiring the skills in a timely way. If he can't, can we move him to another position within the organization in which he does have the needed skills to succeed? If there isn't a position for her in the organization, and if she can't come up to speed in a timely way, we must manage her out of the organization. There simply isn't enough of a match to continue.

We always feel sad about these endings because the person is often hardworking and sincere. But the longer we keep him in a mismatched position, the longer others need to take up the slack and compensate for his inability to do the job.

When Factors Aren't Clear

When a manager has more than one of these four factors mismatched, it can be a lot of work to rehabilitate him. An MMOT gives a person a fair chance to start again and turn over a new leaf. In the end, however, it is up to him to make the grade. And while the MMOT can seem an unwelcome intervention, it is one of the few interventions that actually has a chance to change the manager's pattern.

In the reality of coaching someone, it may not be entirely clear what is missing. On the surface it may appear that interest, attitude, alignment, and skills are all present. Something, though, isn't right. It is necessary in these cases to look at the whole picture and less at the independent variables. There may be something you haven't considered, such as that she doesn't respect or like your method of leadership and management. All statistical studies show that job satisfaction and to some degree job performance are most influenced by a person's direct supervisor. It is a humbling experience but a critical discussion if stylistic differences are affecting your employee's motivation. This situation is surely as much of a mismatch as other combinations. However, it is subtler and harder to talk about. The leader may need to put the subject on the table. This is another learning experience. The leader may not know the impact that he is inadvertently having, and, when explored, he may decide to change some of his leadership style. More often, the issue of leadership style can *become* the issue. When this happens, it prevents the manager from hearing and taking seriously the feedback she is getting. By making my leader's style the point of the MMOT, my responsibility to change gets neutered and prevents real learning and appropriate change from taking place.

That said, stylistic differences can be fundamental and need to be addressed just as we would other elements of the MMOT. Facts of the case need to be acknowledged. "What behaviors are getting in the way of your performance?" Establish a few concrete examples. If the leader acknowledges the stylistic difference, does she agree it is a legitimate barrier to learning? If she agrees, she needs to commit to new performance behaviors. And she needs to be held every bit as accountable—expecting feedback and follow-up as with any other behavior that stands in the way of improved performance. It would not be unusual for both people to learn a great deal in this exchange. However, often the leader doesn't concur that her behavior is a legitimate barrier to the manager's learning. Then the change in orientation falls primarily on the manager's shoulders.

As with other mismatches, ultimately, if you can't agree or change, then one of you has to go. Chances are, the leader will be staying. Yet these conversations can be as enlightening as they are difficult and can lead to new performance on both sides of the equation. That benefits the entire company and changes its culture.

11
Working Within the Strategic Alliance

The MMOT can be used within the context of strategic alliances and subcontractor relationships. Often the process is more complex than it would be with an individual manager or a single team. There are many more "moving parts," more lines of authority to include in the exercise, and more unknowns.

One example of this process occurred between two companies—a high-tech supplier (which we will call ABZ) and an organization that designs and manufactures interface devices for the home electronic entertainment industry (which we will call High Tech Home, HTH).

HTH approached ABZ in 2002 about providing various components for its products. At first ABZ declined the offer. ABZ's CFO said, "The business that HTH would bring to ABZ appeared to undercut important business relationships with customers. We were concerned that our higher-end components would become commoditized and we would create friction between ourselves and our usual customers who make very high-end and pricey products. If ABZ began to advertise it had some of the same components in its less expensive products, we knew we would be in trouble with our customers."

HTH redesigned its original proposal into one in which the potential problems were addressed. ABZ liked the new proposition and agreed to become a strategic partner in this product line. The two organizations began to work together. Very soon, the ABZ people realized that HTH had a lot of systems problems. Accounting practices were not easy to understand in relationship to costs of material, labor, and manufacturing expenses. Both organizations were working against a fixed deadline when a new product line was to be introduced. A $10 million television ad campaign was scheduled to hit in the fall, and now in May, the two organizations were still trying to understand how to integrate their efforts.

Over the first few months of working together, matters seemed to get increasingly worse. "There was smoke everywhere," observed one of ABZ's senior executives, "and we were getting concerned." The organizations set up weekly meetings. The ABZ people would point out various issues. The HTH people were defensive and in denial. For every issue the ABZ people put on the table, the HTH people accused the ABZ people of similar lapses. "We slammed them, because we did do what we said we would do. And any time we didn't do what we said, we would acknowledge it right away and try to give them advance warning," said another ABZ team member.

During the first few meetings the group laid out a number of schedules, defined the outcomes they were after, and put together a tracking system to manage adjustments to the process in a timely way. But matters still got worse.

The ABZ team did a site visit to better analyze what was occurring. "The people we talked with were clueless about how their own processes were supposed to work," said an ABZ team member. "They were overworked and overwhelmed. Many of them were working fourteen hours a day, seven days a week, on this project, and they were at their wits' end."

The ABZ people met some of the teams that were assigned the lion's share of the actual work. These people seemed to be afraid of their senior folks and said yes to their "orders," even though they knew they didn't have the capacity to accomplish the assignments. When they failed to make their due dates, they would "take personal responsibility for it," which in this case meant admitting blame. But these people were powerless to perform any better than they had within the current setup.

The ABZ people decided to have an MMOT meeting with HTH's senior folks. The ABZ people set up a series of "pre-meetings" with some of the managers involved to alert them to the upcoming meeting. One ABZ manager said, "First, we had planned meetings with each of our counterparts at HTH. Frank, a senior manager, talked to the VP of manufacturing and I talked with her boss, a senior vice president, to let them know that we were sending an executive summary regarding our findings from the site visit and that we wanted to have an executive-level discussion." Another ABZ manager said, "The executive summary placed HTH on notice that key issues warranted immediate and urgent resolution. The document was used as a tool to facilitate our discussions and raise the bar on their performance by articulating our expectations for deliverables and accountability."

Another ABZ manager said, "They were all put on formal notice, and by using our documentation we wanted to communicate that we needed their organization to react with the appropriate urgency that the situation warranted."

The first step was to acknowledge reality. The ABZ folks were not out to ambush the HTH team. They also didn't want to have a moan-and-groan meeting in which people would become more defensive than they already were. The ABZ people didn't want to escalate the conflict, but they wanted to engage HTH's team in the process of addressing reality objectively and facing up to the hard issues that could hurt both organizations.

At the meeting, people were ready to address the issues because the ABZ folks had stated them objectively, accurately, and fairly. They were not trying to resolve the difficulties through a problem-solving approach. Rather, they restated the common goals—the product line making its due date—and current reality, which not only included the problems, but also the advances that had been achieved. Using these two data points as the organizing principle, they worked to find ways to put the right systems in place.

The ABZ team addressed reality by illustrating the issues through the use of data templates. They avoided telling anecdotal stories about problems. Soon the HTH team became a partner in understanding reality. The acknowledgment process set the tone, and the HTH people were able to shift from being in denial to actively seeking the truth, even if it made them look bad.

"They weren't used to having a contractor push back as thoughtfully and forcefully as we did," said one of ABZ's managers. "But after a while they came to trust us because we weren't trying to assign blame."

After both sides acknowledged the situation, the group began to analyze how it got to be that way. "We would break down the processes so we could figure out how the organizations performed the ways they did," one of the HTH managers said. "We would track bad processes, orders being misplaced, and data not matching up with other data."

"We came back to the HTH folks and walked through example after example," said one of the ABZ team members. "So we began to create a new plan together. Proper resources were assigned. Product development was behind schedule, so HTH assigned more engineers and gave them strict deliverables and due dates." The group analyzed what they could not change and together transformed the systems in which they worked.

The follow-up phase took the form of weekly feedback meetings, analyzing the current state of the process, action planning, and various adjustments. The teams learned how to work with each other, and by the time the ad campaign went on line, the product was on the shelves.

One of the ABZ managers said, "Our efforts resulted in several key behavioral changes in working with HTH that have enhanced working relationships not only with ABZ, but with all their subcontractors. For example, ABZ suggested ways to improve communications by conducting an all-network subcontractor meeting to inform everyone of program changes, operational issues. This is just one example of how they have taken the lead from ABZ and have experienced positive results."

The Challenges of the Strategic Alliance

Often the senior executive team forms a strategic alliance. Those responsible for the alliance often are ill prepared to integrate both organizations to create a workable relationship. There are crucial authority and accountability issues. Systems do not usually mesh, and the workload and managerial burden becomes so problematic that it seems like the alliance is more effort than it's worth.

People on both sides resent the alliance as cultures and systems continually clash. Well-meaning managers on both sides try to make matters better, but often they simply make matters worse.

The ABZ-HTH example demonstrates many practical lessons. We need to make sure that our house is in order, that we act on behalf of the collective outcome desired, that we explore our own part in critical issues and difficulties, that we tell ourselves the truth within our own organization, and that we explore reality with our partners in the spirit of inquiry.

We may need to have several meetings with each other. Most organizations wait too long to address issues that need to be faced. We should get into the habit of addressing such issues early in the process rather than waiting for a full-fledged confrontation. We need to set the tone and relationship from the start.

Often those who have forged the strategic alliance have not considered the managerial complexity required for things to work well. The manifestations of these complexities are often invisible to the folks who put the deal together. Middle managers do not have the authority to make significant changes to policies or systems, and yet they are the ones charged with the deliverables. Of course, they feel powerless and resentful to be put in such a position.

Managerial moments of truth move not only downward within the organization but upward as well. Often managers need to drive reality up to the decision makers when they do not have the authority to change the fundamentals that make the alliance unworkable. Facing reality is everyone's job. No one can know the whole picture. We need to put the fragments together to see reality. This is a collective act, although it is also an act of leadership. Those in leadership positions must demand that information flow upward as well as downward. They must insist that the fragments be analyzed, understood systemically and structurally, and that this understanding is used as the basis of change and adjustment.

The ABZ-HTH story is an example of how people were seeking to communicate on a number of levels and to put the results of those communications together. While it would have been easier and certainly more "natural" to blame others, the MMOT enabled the ABZ team to engage with the HTH team in ways that were penetrating and exceedingly productive, and set the stage for a long-term professional relationship that fulfilled the original intent behind the strategic alliance.

12

Rules of Thumb

Timing

When is the right time for a managerial moment of truth? The rule of thumb is to choose a period when you have time to adequately cover the issues at hand, rather than be forced to abruptly halt the conversation halfway through. When possible, set the agenda in advance: *The agenda for tomorrow's meeting is to address the recent quality issues.*

Another rule of thumb is to conduct the MMOT close to the events that will be covered, while they're fresh in everyone's mind. If we talk about events that occurred weeks or months ago, much relevant information may have been forgotten, and we lose the impact of exploring important managerial subject matter.

Conducting an MMOT meeting while a manager is in the midst of leading an initiative is often more effective than waiting until the project cycle is entirely complete. If we have doubts or perceive a "disturbance in the force" within a team, process, or project, it may be time to have a meeting. We may have formed a wrong impression, and checking in puts our mind to rest. Or we may discover something that might have turned out badly had we not addressed it at this very point in the process.

The Rule of Thumb Is: Be Direct

The spirit in which we conduct MMOTs is to be clear and straightforward in ways that are effective and accessible to the individual we are addressing. We often need to learn how to be more direct and objective than we are used to, so it might seem strange at first. As you will see, directness is compatible with supportiveness and good manners.

During the late 1980s and early 1990s, many managers were taught a technique called "pillow-punch-pillow." This is a form of indirectly delivering news that makes managers uncomfortable. Here's an example we may recognize:

"You know, you're one of the most talented engineers we've had here, and I'm really glad you're part of the team. But this cost override has caused us a lot of problems, and you have to watch it more carefully. However, nonetheless, I really think the work was brilliant, and you and your team did an outstanding job."

Pillow: You're wonderful.
Punch: You went over budget, you idiot.
Pillow: You and the team are brilliant.

The pillow-punch-pillow approach never works well because, by trying to soften the blow, the manager can be seen as disingenuous. When you are on the receiving end of pillow-punch-pillow, it can feel like you are being dealt a slow hand at a crooked game of seven-card stud. The best policy is to be direct:

"I want to talk to you about the costs for this project."

When the Matter You Are Addressing Is Imprecise

A good rule of thumb is to understand exactly the situation you are addressing. Sometimes, there is something we want to address, but it is hard to find the right words, or the precise example, or the appropriate specifics. We should try to address it anyway.

If our previous MMOT meetings with this manager have been successful, and we have a good relationship with this person, it is easier to try to talk about those things that are hard to define but are factors we want to address. We can enter into a collaborative exploration in the spirit of truth. We want to avoid vague complaints that the person can't understand or address. We may say:

"I want to talk about your approach to the Goodwin account. Now, I'm not able to put my finger on exactly what I'm sensing, but let's spend a few minutes talking about it, and maybe you can help me find a way to get at what I'm sensing."

Actor Charlton Heston gave this example of an unclear moment of truth in his professional life. During the first few days of shooting *Ben-Hur*, director William Wyler came to Heston and told him, "Chuck, you're not good enough in this part. You have to be better. If I knew how to tell you how to be better, I would. But I don't. The only thing I can say is you have to be better."

Along with *Raintree County*, shot a few years before, *Ben-Hur* was the only other film that was shot on the highly expensive 65 mm negative stock but printed on 70 mm prints intended for projection containing additional space for stereophonic tracks that were printed in magnetic strips directly on the film, providing four channels of stereo sound, which was a major technical advancement in 1959. With superstars in the leading roles and a cast of more than fifteen thousand extras, the film was the most expensive to that date. Both Heston and Wyler knew the stakes. MGM had bet the farm on this film. If it didn't succeed, the studio would have to go into receivership and eventually bankruptcy.

And now Heston, playing the title role, was told by his director that he wasn't making it and that he had to figure out how to be better. Heston did some soul searching and dedicated himself to being better than he knew how to be. He rose to the occasion, turning in a stellar performance that won him the Academy Award for best actor. The film went on to be a financial success and a classic, winning a total of eleven Academy Awards.

What if William Wyler had not said what he did to Heston?

Although he didn't know how to give Heston specific suggestions, Wyler needed to let Heston know where he stood. All of the crew was concerned about the film's success and the dire consequences if they failed. They didn't have the luxury to misrepresent reality to each other.

Sometimes we need to address a managerial moment of truth, even though we can't cite chapter and verse about the situation we are addressing. While those can be the most difficult conversations because we can't isolate exactly what we are trying to address, it may be critical to tackle this moment of truth anyway. Still, we need to understand that a conversation around issues we can't pinpoint can be fraught with danger. We can be misunderstood, and the good we are trying to achieve may be lost in the resulting confusion. This is why building trust over time enables us to have the type of professional relationship in which such impressionistic explorations are given and taken in good faith. The rule of thumb: use your managerial common sense and proceed with caution.

The Pitcher, the Catcher, and the Manager

When the manager of a baseball team asks the catcher, "How's the pitcher doing?," the catcher must tell the manager the truth. If the catcher tells the manager that the pitcher is doing better than is true, the manager has to get a new catcher.

We need to know how our direct reports' managers are doing. One of Blue Shield of California's leadership principles is *Know your people and your people's people*. What are they like? What are their capabilities and talents? What are their challenges and areas of development? How are they as individual performers and team members?

Most MMOTs occur between a manager and her direct report. Yet the manager's boss might also be involved *indirectly*. A good rule of thumb is that it is important for everyone involved in the broader management system to have a sense of how people are doing throughout the organization. What is the plan for organizational growth and individual professional development? This question enables us to better understand and build our human resource capacity. Seen from a broader vantage point, we want to consider the overall growth of our organizational competence.

Core Competence and Organizational Learning

The rule of thumb is this: use the MMOTs to enable us to develop the organization's core competencies.

Gary Hamel and C. K. Prahalad coined the term *core competence*, which unfortunately has become corporate jargon. Too often the phrase has been used to mean simple *competence*, as in, "Joe's core competence is in his ability to look at a spreadsheet." The way that Hamel and Prahalad meant the term is very different. They say an organization's core competence is one of their most strategic assets. They argue that *it takes over one hundred people within the organization having the same level of competence to describe the company as having a true core competence.* "If only a few people have competence in an area, they can walk out the door and leave the company cold. The organization doesn't have a core competence if a few people could take it away," Hamel has said.

A good rule of thumb is to work with two important ideas: *core competencies* and *the learning organization.* Although both ideas have suffered "jargonization," these are powerful notions—an organization's actual special abilities that give it the unique facility to advance its mission, and the organization's ability to learn how to add these very competencies.

Organizational learning is not simply *individuals* within an organization *learning.* The engineers in many high-tech companies spend much of their time learning: how to design software, or work within certain programs, or develop new motherboards. Too often, the learning doesn't become assimilated into the organization, and other engineers have to discover the very same information on their own.

The difference between that type of situation and a true learning organization is this: *the learning organization has the ability to pass the learning on to the collective whole.* Once someone develops a new competency, it can enter into the knowledge base of the entire organization. Learning *and* developing competencies go hand in hand. Without organizational learning, the company cannot change, add, develop, or advance. Without adequate core competencies, the company will not be able to implement its strategies, grow its markets, and develop its business opportunity. The advantages the company enjoys today could be gone tomorrow if a few people left.

The MMOT serves both causes. We learn and develop competencies through a clear understanding of what we want to accomplish, where we are in relation to our goals, and a dynamic learning process that enables us to invent new systems and approaches to accomplish our aims.

The MMOT is essentially a learning process. While we do want to correct substandard performance, that alone will not help us increase capacity. We want to use the MMOT to enter into a dialogue within a larger learning context. A good rule of thumb is to ask ourselves these critical questions:

- What are we learning?
- How are we learning?
- How are we establishing this learning relationship?
- What generalized principles can we learn and then apply elsewhere?
- How can we spread this learning to others?
- How can we be more efficient at identifying learning moments and capitalizing on them?

The Quick MMOT

While we have been suggesting a full process of the four-step MMOT technique for addressing managerial moments of truth, there is also room for the quick MMOTs. These may take place in a matter of minutes. Here is an example of an MMOT that quickly follows the four-step process:

"Did you get the contract back from Allied Inc.?"

"Not yet."

"When did we say we wanted it back?"

"The fourth."

"It's now the seventh. What's going on?"

"Their lawyer made some changes that our lawyers are reviewing."

"What can we do to speed up the process?"

"Manage our own lawyers."

"Will you do that?"

"Yes. I'll tell them to expedite their review."

"It seems to me we have had these delays before. Is there anything we can do about it?"

"I need to manage our lawyers better."

"What will you do differently?"

"Call them more often to drive the due dates."

"Will that get us the result?"

"I think so."

"Let me know how it's working out."

"Okay."

This dialogue almost seems like a normal managerial conversation. But there are a few significant MMOT factors involved. Reality is acknowledged and analyzed. A new plan is put into place. The conversation even ends with a feedback system—"Let me know how it's working out"—albeit an informal one. Quick meetings of this sort are very effective when you need to make small adjustments in the process. These adjustments are often helpful and add support to the process.

An important rule of thumb is to let the amount of time you give a meeting be determined by the nature of the difference between the desired result and the actual result. If we try to use a quick MMOT process in areas that are critical and chronic, we will not be able to support the type of change necessary. Yet the quick MMOT has an important role in our strategy of addressing managerial moments of truth early on in the management process, where small changes can avert the need for larger confrontations down the line.

Timeliness Versus Burning Platform

A bit of organizational jargon is the *burning platform*, an image that captures a sense of life-threatening urgency. The phrase comes from an initiative game in which participants are standing on a platform. As part of the game, they are told that the platform is burning and they have to save all of their team members. They must devise ways to leave the burning platform without any members being lost in the fire.

In fact, people do have a real sense of urgency when reality calls for it. If the fire were real, people would understand the actual conditions and act with a sense of urgency. Great managers understand when and how to move faster because the situation demands it.

The burning platform type of managerial trick, however, consistently backfires. *Reality is the only foundation on which we can base our quest to improve performance.* If in reality there are reasons we must get on with it quickly and forcefully, then we are well motivated to act accordingly, and any sense of urgency we have is caused by the actual situation. No one has to convince the staff at the emergency ward in the hospital to act with a sense of urgency. They act that way because they are facing real emergencies. Good managers understand the difference between situations that call for urgency and ones that do not.

Rather than attempt to motivate people through fiction, we can manage them through fact. Rather than try to create a sense of urgency artificially, *we can create a sense of timeliness.*

When we understand what has to happen and by when, including the relationships that each goal has with other goals, we will have the exact sense of urgency that is appropriate to the actual reality we are managing. A genuine sense of urgency is driven by a desire for competitive excellence on behalf of organizational greatness. The best way of describing this is an acute sense of timeliness.

The rule of thumb, then, is this: *have a sense of timeliness.* Do not try to create a sense of urgency artificially. This is another variation on the theme of *tell the truth.* While we may not have considered the degree to which creating a false sense of urgency is a distortion of reality, in the long run it works against our ability to create an organization that is capable and inclined to see and tell the truth.

Deadlines

The rule of thumb is *use deadlines to organize events in time,* rather than to pressure people into action. Deadlines help the manager set priorities and schedule accordingly.

Deadlines can be one of the most effective organizing tools. But too often deadlines are not used well. Many MMOTs are about missed deadlines. However, the adjustments to the process often do not lead to a basic shift in understanding how to use deadlines well and what to avoid.

If we need to ship the product on October 14, we can design a schedule of events that enables us to know by when we need to get the materials delivered, the line ready for manufacturing, the boxes printed, the product assembled and boxed, the date the marketing campaign begins to run, the date the sales staff needs to be introduced to the new product, and so on. These events do not call for pressure. They call for managerial mastery of scheduling, sequencing, and contingency planning. They call for understanding the relationships of the parts to the whole and for organizing events in time, and ultimately, for understanding what it takes to meet the commitment.

The shift from deadlines as pressure points to deadlines as events to manage within a timely system is profound. The world changes and deadlines become aids in a complex process, rather than events to dread.

Part of the shift is to enable the manager to move from a "to-do list" mentality to one in which she is seeing the project from a greater sense of perspective, able to see and understand the entire shape of the project and how the details fit into the picture.

This shift is consistent with the thrust of the MMOT. By using the tool of the MMOT, we are learning how to enable our teams to back up, see a broader picture, and understand relationships and what causes what. The "to-do list" mind-set forces us to experience time in short, unrelated episodes. When we back up, our experience of time changes. We begin to see longer time frames, which gives us more control over the events we are managing.

Compliance to Alignment

Another rule of thumb is to work toward team and individual alignment, not simply compliance. If we consistently work with the four steps of the MMOT, our managers will be capable of greater performance. But we need to understand that there is a difference between improved performance as a product of compliance and improved performance that is an outcome of alignment. Compliance is a response to circumstances, while alignment is self-generating. Our level of involvement tells the story. We comply with rules that others set, but our involvement is limited. When we align, we drive our own choices to be involved fully.

If we are simply using an MMOT to change behavior, we will often see people complying rather than aligning with the organization and its aims. When we use an MMOT as part of a broader mentoring process, we are more apt to inspire alignment because we explore the match between the person's values and aspirations and those of the enterprise.

Truth telling, more than any other factor, creates alignment for the individual and team. It is not enough to favor common goals and visions for the future. Many people agree with their organization's vision and goals, but they are not aligned with the organization. Alignment, as we have said, is not always agreement. Out of alignment, we might drive issues, challenge data and assumptions, rethink processes, and put differences of opinion on the table to discuss. But once decisions are made, even if they are not the ones we might have made, we roll up our sleeves and make the decisions work.

Building alignment does not occur in one or two events, but happens over an extended period of time based on how the organization consistently manages itself. An organization that is doing meaningful work, respects its members, is able to learn, and is able to tell the truth builds alignment. Consistent patterns of behavior are key. Alignment does not demand perfection. We can make mistakes. Alignment does demand learning, common values and goals, truth telling, and a fair process.

Genuine Commitment to Drive: Design/Policy Issues Up to the Decision Makers

One of the most frustrating experiences managers have is to be on the short end of ill-conceived policies or poorly designed processes. A high percentage of chronic organizational dysfunction originates from these types of design issues. Often, when analyzing how the performance turned out as it did, managers discover that the processes in which they had to work were not capable of producing the results for which they were accountable.

A software company decided to introduce a new software accounting product that was meant to replace their current highly popular accounting package. Senior management had ordered the new package but failed to take into account why the current program was so popular. They had outsourced the development of the new product, but the developers did not understand how to re-create the features of the older product, which was developed by another subcontractor no longer in business. The senior managers decided to go ahead, thinking that they needed to show the market that they were upgrading their offering. The packaging was radically changed with glossy graphics and splashy animation, and they advertised the new release. Since the new product wasn't as good as the older product, the new release bombed. The sales force was put on notice to increase sales. But the word was on the street that the new release didn't measure up to the old one. The older product became a hot item on eBay, which made the new product look even worse.

The sales force couldn't sell the new product, and the older product had been taken off the market. Since they were not authorized to decide what products the company would release, they needed to drive the situation upward to the senior team. In fact, at first the senior team thought that the salespeople didn't know how to sell the new product, and it was not because of the quality of the software package itself, but that any new product would have been met with resistance. In a meeting with senior staff, the sales team demonstrated both products side by side and showed polls that indicated that their customers thought the new product was inferior. Finally, they opened the eBay site that was selling the old package. The copy that people had written made the older program seem like an invaluable accounting miracle and the newer product a dud.

The senior team had a decision to make. While they had put their reputation on the line with the new product, they knew they were losing market credibility. They put the older product back on the market, called it "classic," and revised the new product until it was better than the original, which took over a year.

Managers need to bring reality to the attention of those who make the decisions. Too often, senior managers create policies and make decisions that create unintended negative consequences. Managers who are charged with making these decisions work find that they can't succeed, no matter what they do. These people are not in a position to make matters better, because design issues are causing the difficulties, and these managers are not authorized to change policies. When this is the case, the rule of thumb is: *always drive matters to those who have the authority to make the decisions.*

A variation on this theme is reported by consultant John Donovan of Donovan Associates, Hanover, New Hampshire, who has worked in large organizations for years. He understands the need for truth telling throughout organizations and has helped many senior teams learn how to be more direct and truthful with each other. Here is a recent experience he had in challenging a team to face reality directly with their CEO.

"A select group of managers from a leading pharmaceutical company was asked by the CEO to redesign the R&D group to more rapidly get products to market. During the initial off-site, the work group created a new integrated design for implementation. They thought it was pretty good. But just a few minutes into their presentation to the CEO, he stood up and quickly and spontaneously drafted his own model. He then asked the group to go off and perfect his model.

"At the next off-site meeting the group struggled all morning to understand and work with the CEO's model. Try as they would, the model didn't make a lot of sense.

"This was a company that was very hierarchical. Once a senior person, especially the CEO, gave what seemed like marching orders, the teams marched in lockstep. Usually in similar situations, teams would figure out compromises so as not to offend the senior person or be seen as critical. They came to realize that the CEO's draft model would not work effectively—his structure was based on setting up completely separate companies—a way of operating that had worked at the company in the '90s but, now, in today's more regulatory, fast-paced environment, would have created excessive bureaucracy, delays, complexity, and barriers between the different functions of Research and Development.

"By early afternoon, they were convinced that the CEO's idea could not serve the original intent of creating a fast-track system for new drugs to make it to the market. In fact, it looked like it would slow things down. The team members had a moment of truth when they admitted to each other what they were seeing.

"After some discussion, the team decided to go back to the CEO and tell him what they thought and why they thought it," Donovan explains. "They set up a meeting the next day.

"A meeting like this was very unusual in this organization, and the group didn't know if they were about to open a can of worms. But they decided that they needed to address the issue squarely because time-to-market was such a critical factor in the company's business strategy.

"The CEO listened to the presentation and saw their point of view. He agreed with much of what they had said, but he also had some factors in mind that they did not address. The group saw his points and went back to design a process and system that would accommodate all of the points they now agreed to.

"The group went back to work with this new awareness and wisely incorporated the CEO's idea. They further developed their original design and developed a new, flexible, streamlined structure that would be capable of ensuring a more rapid development of new products. Subsequently, their presentation of this new hybrid model was a resounding success. This would not have happened as well if the team had not decided to have a moment of truth with the CEO, and if the CEO had not engaged in exploring the issues the team had identified."

Make the MMOT Your Own

You have your own style, your own voice, your own personality, level of experience, and rhythm. This book comes alive when you add your own managerial intelligence to the MMOT principles and then put them into practice. Each situation is unique, as is each person and team you manage.

Each relationship you develop is unlike any other. Each person has different potentials, aspirations, values, skills, personality, and rhythms. There is room within the organization for these differences as long as the job requirements are satisfied. We are not cogs in a wheel. We are individuals who have chosen to join an organization so that we can add our talents, efforts, energy, creativity, skills, judgment, time, and support on behalf of the success and well-being of the company.

While every member of the organization may be accountable for common standards, such as level of performance, attitude, outcomes, values, alignment, professional stance, and so on, it is the fact that our own unique individual stamp has a place within the organization that enables it to reach true greatness.

The rule of thumb is: *make every MMOT your own.*

A Final Word

How easy it is to fall into old habits. How challenging it is to learn how to travel a new path. We mean well, but then we get busy. Our New Year's resolutions, so sincerely made and well meant, are often a memory by February. People say it's hard to change one's ways. People say it's especially hard for the organization. Fads come and go; new mottos appear as old ones disappear. New practices regularly hit the scene: Excellence, Quality, Business Process Reengineering, Six Sigma, Balanced Scorecard, and on and on it goes. The latest popular practices come with new jargon replacing old jargon, and most people hope this time the change will take hold. Too often, it is gone before we know it.

Yet change itself is not the enigma it seems. Nor does it always slip away. Change that is well motivated lasts and builds on itself. When we think about the Internet, computerization, word processing, e-mail, miniaturization, BlackBerrys, TiVo, and teleconferencing, we can see how easily change can be adopted, how it can last, how fast it can become integrated into our lives. Changes in the last twenty years have dramatically revolutionized how we conduct business, distribute our products and services, reach the market, engage with customers, and forge our own futures. We all understand that the speed of changing circumstances is now faster than ever before in history. But few organizations are truly disciplined in understanding and adapting to this global momentum. Organizations are structured to deal with the predictable, the repeatable, the traditions, the common practice. This is one of the great strengths of the organization. However, it also can be its fatal weakness if that's all it can do. Now there is another equally important discipline that has become an organizational imperative, and that is the ability to understand the times and adapt as needed. This often means change must happen long before we are ready for it.

Our mind-set, or orientation, is one of the key factors in our ability to understand how reality may have changed and what we need to do about it. It is human and natural to see our own neck of the woods as if that were the larger world. But, fortunately, we also have the ability to see beyond our instinctive limitations and to understand that we live in a much bigger and more connected world. The essence of the organization is the interconnectedness of the parts to a comprehensive whole. We do not actually work in isolation, although too often people feel they do. This feeling often drives people to think about the organization as competing parts that work against each other, rather than integrated critical elements that are coordinated to make the whole greater than the sum of the parts.

When we can't tell each other the truth as directly and accurately as we need to, the organization further fragments into isolated sectors as managers feel forced to create even more protection for themselves and their teams. This is a cycle that creates its own strange universe, one in which people unknowingly collude in managing how much truth can and cannot be told.

The MMOT offers an approach to truth telling that is a direct means to performance improvement. But in a larger sense, it is planting seeds that can change the landscape of the modern organization. An organization that can seek a real understanding of the reality it faces must be capable and practiced in telling itself the truth enterprise-wide. An organization that assesses reality quickly and accurately has a distinct competitive advantage, and the key to determining what the circumstances are and how they are changing is inextricably tied to truth telling.

As a manager, using the MMOT consistently when the situation calls for it will increase your actual capacity and shift the managerial burden more equitably. The people you work with will improve their performances, their sense of alignment, and their relationships with each other and with you. Another benefit can occur as well. The organization as a collective body can come to realize the deeper value of truth, both as a practical managerial practice and as a force around which people can align. Information can then flow more easily and readily to where it needs to go within the organization. Everyone benefits when truth becomes the foundation for the type of predictability *and* flexibility so needed in today's business environment.

Once people have a taste for truth telling, it doesn't go away. While it's challenging and difficult at times, it also is a powerful agent of change. Once the manager has had a few successful experiences using the MMOT working to improve performance and managers' capabilities, she will want to use it again rather than live with substandard performance. The MMOT helps the manager clear the air, which itself makes matters better. More importantly, it gives people the very best chance to learn, improve, become better at their professions, and develop their capabilities, value to the organization, and careers. People realize that all the manipulations and other compensating actions of avoiding the truth are a lot more work than just facing reality. After a while, they recognize that it takes less time and effort to create a management team capable of finding and telling the truth than to lead a team that avoids it. Our appreciation of the MMOT is not hopefulness based on theory, but the conclusion we have come to because of our real-world experience.

Our experience with organizations that have taken on the MMOT approach has been exciting and gratifying. The process seems to take on a life of its own, and managers take it to heart, both in spirit and in practice. We begin to see them try it out, practice it, evaluate how well it works, put in their own adjustments, and then adopt it as standard operating procedure. The MMOT technique made situations that would be usually difficult to face approachable and accessible. Now, when a manager says to a person or a team,

"We need to have a moment of truth," more often than not the response is, "Okay, let's really look at reality together." People take it as a serious event that helps them communicate, improve, and further align their efforts.

The practical value of the form for the MMOT makes truth telling more available. We are not dedicated to the four-step form as such. But we can observe how useful it is. Most organizations have a list of value statements that include "honesty" or "truth" or "integrity." These words are on the list because that's what people throughout the organization want. But how to put these values into practice? That has always been the hard nut to crack. We like the MMOT process because it gives managers a simple form to use so their chances of success increase. Sometimes we need to know just how to do what we want to do. The key is to find an approach that works. And for it to really work, we mean the outcome must be significant. We may not always achieve the results we want, but it gives us the very best chance to do so.

As we have emphasized, the result we want is not simply corrections to behavior, but rather the full manifestation of the people's potential. We want that for ourselves as well. While the MMOT is often led by one person for another or for a team, it is a mutual moment of truth and learning for everyone. Some of what is learned is obvious, such as performance patterns, process design and execution, planning, managing. But some of the lessons learned are harder to list with such tangible clarity. There are human questions to consider such as, How can we bring out the best in each other? How can we reach beyond our usual range? How can we be better at what we do, at how we manage, at how we learn, at how we work together, and how we cocreate with each other? How can we, together, build a great organization?

We suggest that you try out the MMOT practice in small and simple situations first. Dedicate yourself to the follow-through. Do not try to be perfect. Allow yourself to make mistakes. Learn from those mistakes. Gain strength over time. And, of course, as we have emphasized many times in this book, *be consistent*. If you are, that sends a message that you mean to be a champion for truth telling.

And finally, the MMOT approach is not only a learning tool, it is a leadership principle. When you take it on, you become a more effective leader as well as a more effective manager. Superior leadership in an organization has a transforming impact. It can change the nature of how well a company can become *its own* predominant creative force, shaping its destiny and the good it can do in the world.

Acknowledgments

Many people have contributed their talents, insights, wisdom, and energy to this book. We are grateful to them all.

Thank you, Jacques de Spoelberch, friend and literary agent, for your untiring support for this book. Over the years and through many book projects, your wisdom and mentorship have been a source of strength and light.

And thank you, Fred Hills, senior editor and champion of this book. It was Fred's vision that brought this book to Simon & Schuster, and his ongoing insight and advice, always perceptive, discerning, and sensitive to the book's thesis, made this project a great pleasure and true learning experience.

And thank you, Peter Senge, friend and colleague, for your words of practical and profound wisdom that you expressed so beautifully in the foreword.

And thank you, Blue Shield of California, an organization that is a model for the thesis of this book. Special thanks go to Blue Shield's Marianne Jackson, senior vice president of Human Resources; Kathy Richards, director of Learning and Development who led the Managerial Moment of Truth training effort for the organization; and her staff, Shannon Rice and Souvanny Philavong. Thank you, Gina Stassi, Bill Brown, Paul Swenson, Betsy Stone, Janet Widmann, Doug Grant, and Tony Verna for your insights, research, and experience in the MMOT technique that you so skillfully contributed to this book. Thank you, Seth Jacobs, for your role in making sure all of our legal contracts were in place, on time, and in English. Thank you, Diann Rose and Leslie Monahan, for your logistical and professional support during this project. Your management of manuscript version control, coast to coast, was a thing of beauty.

Thank you, Lisa Delmar and Leslie Bianchi of Robert Fritz, Inc. Your dedication and untiring work on behalf of this book have been remarkable. And thank you, Beth Massiano, Robert Fritz, Inc., consultant, who worked directly with Blue Shield in developing the MMOT training, and for leading the instructor trainings for BSC.

Thank you, Tom Epstein, for your keen eye in reviewing the manuscript.

Thank you, John Donovan, William Brandt, and Tom Flanagan, for your contribution to the manuscript.

And thank you, Edith Lewis and Patty Romanowski Bashe, for your exceptional editorial support.

And from Bruce: My special thanks to the senior staff of Blue Shield of California. Your positive involvement in the very first training of MMOT led to our conviction that this technique could change the quality of manager and organizational performance. Working with you to bring leadership excellence to Blue Shield has been a privilege.

And from Robert: Thank you, Rosalind, beloved wife, who is the center of my life, friend, lover, colleague, partner, co-explorer, master structural consultant, and president of Robert Fritz, Inc. Your support moves me beyond words.

You may reach Robert Fritz at:

Robert Fritz, Inc.
P.O. Box 189
Newfane, VT 05345
Telephone: (800) 848-9700
(802) 365-7286
Fax: (802) 365-7285
E-mail: info@robertfritz.com

Visit our Web site at www.robertfritz.com for a schedule of events and news, and to receive our monthly newsletter.

Mr. Bruce Bodaken may be contacted for further information about the issues described in his book, or to arrange speaking engagements, at:

MOT@blueshieldca.com

About the Authors

BRUCE BODAKEN is chairman, president, and CEO of Blue Shield of California, a 3.3-million member not-for-profit health plan that serves the commercial, individual, and government markets in California. He earned a master's degree and taught philosophy at the college level before embarking on a career in health care.

During Mr. Bodaken's five-year tenure as CEO, Blue Shield has been one of the fastest-growing health plans in California. Membership has more than doubled, and company revenues have risen from $3 billion to $7 billion plus. In the past three years, the company won vigorous competitions for two large government contracts, covering more than 400,000 state employees in CalPERS and half a million members of U.S. military families enrolled in the TRICARE program.

Passionate about his company's not-for-profit mission, Mr. Bodaken is the first health plan CEO to offer a specific proposal to cover all Californians. His provocative plan for universal coverage based on universal responsibility has earned praise from major news organizations throughout the country. During his tenure, he also transformed the Blue Shield of California Foundation into one of the state's largest health-care grantmakers, with nearly $30 million in donations planned for 2005. Most of the foundation's grants support programs to help the uninsured or combat domestic violence.

In addition to his work at Blue Shield, Mr. Bodaken serves on numerous professional and civic boards. He is a member of the board of directors of Wage Works, the California Business Roundtable, America's Health Insurance Plans, and the University of California, Berkeley's Health Services Management Program. He is also a member of the UCSF School of Pharmacy Dean's Board of Advisors.

For more than twenty years, ROBERT FRITZ has been developing the field of structural dynamics through his work, first in the area of the creative process and then in the area of organizational, business, and management issues. He is the founder of Robert Fritz, Inc., and, along with Peter Senge and Charlie Kiefer, Innovation Associates.

Fritz began to lead courses in the creative process as applied to personal effectiveness in the mid-1970s. He then trained others to lead his courses, and now more than eighty thousand people have participated in these trainings throughout the world.

His first major book on the relationship of structure to human behavior was *The Path of Least Resistance*, followed by *Creating*, *Corporate Tides*, *The Path of Least Resistance for Managers*, and *Your Life as Art*. These books, along with his trainings, have introduced revolutionary ideas about the influence of structural causality on human beings, both as individuals and within organizations.

As a consultant, Fritz has helped many organizations put the structural approach into practice, and his clients include Fortune 500 companies, many midsize companies, as well as governmental and nonprofit organizations. Working with other structural consultants, Robert Fritz, Inc., is in the forefront of revolutionary change in how organizations structure themselves to produce sustained high performance.

Fritz began the study of structure as a composition student at the Boston Conservatory of Music in the 1960s. Later, he studied composition in Germany and was on the faculty of the New England Conservatory of Music and Berklee College. After receiving his BM and MM in composition, Fritz worked as a studio musician in New York and Hollywood, and won positions in *Playboy* and *Downbeat* magazine readers' polls. Fritz continues to be an active composer and has written film scores, operas, symphonic music, and chamber music. Most recently, Fritz also directs films, documentaries, and television programs.